The Living Fire:

SELECTED POEMS OF LEO E. O'NEIL 1973-1997

SELECTED AND EDITED, WITH AN INTRODUCTION BY
RAY GAMACHE

Cover design and section heads by Charlie Lemay,
Manchester, New Hampshire

Back cover photo of Bishop O'Neil courtesy of Cote
Photography, Manchester, New Hampshire

Published by Wayfarer Press, Box 609, Bethlehem,
New Hampshire 03574

Printed in the United States of America by Sant Bani
Press, Tilton, New Hampshire. Printed on 60 lb.
Exact Offset Opaque Natural Vellum Finish paper,
manufactured in Groveton by Wausau Papers of New
Hampshire. Paper in part provided by the generosity
of St. Francis Xavier Parish, Groveton, and Sacred
Heart Parish, North Stratford, New Hampshire

Book Design by Ray Gamache

"The Passion According to St. Matthew," taken from *J.S. Bach: Choral Works*, G. Schirmer, Inc., New York, New York

The New Revised Standard Version has been used to cite
biblical allusions throughout.

ISBN 0-9646061-2-7

CONTENTS

An introduction to the poetry of Leo E. O'Neil

To the people of western Massachusetts and New Hampshire, Leo E. O'Neil (1928-1997), the first Auxiliary Bishop of Springfield and the eighth Bishop of Manchester, needs little or no biographical introduction. That he was beloved as parish priest, pastor and bishop has been chronicled by both the religious and popular presses. That he was a storyteller extraordinaire, a raconteur, was also known by many people who had the opportunity to engage him in his ministry. The story was that he even wrote an occasional poem. To what extent he used poetry and how accomplished a poet he was have heretofore not been established. However, that story is substantiated and some of those questions are answered in this, the first published volume of his poetry.

The catalogue of Bishop O'Neil's collected poetry includes one-hundred and forty poems, which total over thirteen hundred manuscript pages. Numbers aside, the argument for a book of poetry grew directly out of the poems themselves. Bishop O'Neil wrote these poems because he decided to use poetry to express himself in his vocation as a priest. It became his rhetorical model of choice, the vehicle in which he was most completely himself, standing out as his most eloquent, comforting, challenging, direct and enchanting work. Bishop O'Neil's poetry is a living symbol of the ministry he lived, and the poems serve as legacy of a man who celebrated the gift of life in each day, each person, each poem.

The earliest evidence is a poem for Father's Day in 1973, which Bishop O'Neil called "a doggerel...to present a humorous change for a sermon and to attempt to be less boring for Father on his day." Although somewhat embarrassed by the poem, "it might be good for my humility to print..." While serving as a priest of the diocese of Springfield in the 1970s, he wrote a few poems, most notably "My Parish," "Reed of God," and "With Trills of Tenderness," which show him working in traditional poetic frameworks.

Shortly before his appointment as first Auxiliary Bishop of Springfield was announced in June 1980, he commemorated two important occasions with poetry. The first was a St. Patrick's Day Mass at which he celebrated the women of Holyoke, who "give the only / gift / that can break the / harshness of a mill city / their gentle, untiring, enduring love." Not surprisingly what prompted the second effort was the twenty-fifth anniversary of ordination for Reverend John F. Burke, his very close friend from the Grand Seminary in Montreal, Quebec, Canada. In both poems, his style takes on much of what would become its chief characteristics: simplicity of structure, thematic weaving of personal and scriptural stories, use of figurative language and oratorical devices. The Burke poem became the template for other occasions involving priests, including "The Sacrament of Friendship," which elucidates one of his key thematic points about the priest's role. "The priest is the storyteller, / the poet, / who tells again and again / in many and varied ways / the promise, / 'Behold I am with you always.'"

By 1981, Bishop O'Neil was regularly writing poems for many occasions which he was called upon to officiate, including Sister Katherine Hinga's final vows on June 6, Father Tom Delehanty's fortieth anniversay on June 7, and Sister Esther Maria's retirement party on June 9. All three poems show lines that are stark and vertical, with few indentations. He begins the poem about Sr. Hinga with a favorite Gospel story from Luke: "All of us / have / walked / Emmaus roads / where / scorching suns / relentlessly / caked / our weariness / and / dusty trees / reflected / our / wilted spirits." These poems reveal that not only had he found his thematic wellspring — religious life requiring a steadfast conviction in the face of a changing cultural landscape — but that he was also becoming more comfortable with a verse form that raged down the page "like a riptide of energy...and spun whirlpools / of words and images / that sprung / in frenzied dance / into our souls."

Throughout the 1980s, Bishop O'Neil continued to hone and explore the possibilities of his craft. He could be completely expansive as in "The Quiet Men of Holyoke," in which he celebrated an entire generation of men, or completely personal as in the many eulogies he delivered for the people in his beloved Holyoke and the four counties of western Massachusetts. In the eulogies, Bishop O'Neil uses the person's name to great effect, creating melodies from roots that he knew and understood so well. He takes us deep into the heart "of old neighborhoods and honorable ancestors" to sing about "the scars of origin," which we must never forget. That, of course, meant his own Irish heritage. In "The Quiet Men," he weaves the biblical story of the Prodigal Son with the Irish song "Danny Boy" to create a parable about the men he watched growing up whose language "was a deeper / clearer thing." The father watches a son depart "until his back / is just a speck / in the soft Erin evening. / And then, / all his unsobbed sobs / and unspoken words / mingle in the shroud / of Irish mist." Ultimately, Bishop O'Neil implores his listeners to make more of this 1983 St. Patrick's Day parade. "Your march / through their / streets / is memorial to them. / Build it again / in their honor." The message in this and many poems is that life must be built upon love, honor and respect for God and one another.

When Pope John Paul II appointed Bishop O'Neil Coadjutor Bishop of Manchester in 1989, he arrived with the characteristics of a mature, confident voice, capable of figurative flights tempered with the fervor and zeal of his mission. Thus, at his own welcoming ceremony, on November 30, 1989, Bishop O'Neil delivered an Advent reflection that must have hit a chord with his New Hampshire listeners which doubtlessly included many of French-Canadian ancestry. Thus, he sprinkles the Blessed Mary's story with phrases in French: "Mere de Dieu...Je vous salue, Marie...Pleine de grace..." However difficult it was to leave his home in Massachusetts, Bishop O'Neil sought no pity, only that Mary "singe our hesitant / hearts / with the same / consuming consent / His will be done / in us." He speaks about the grandeur of God forever etched in New Hampshire's forests, lakes, cities, villages, ocean, mountains, and how the faith of this people is "granite solid, / ridged and forged / to the Rock of Peter." He asks that the Church in New Hampshire "ignite once more / the fire within / us to be heralds / of cross / and resurrection." Bishop O'Neil carried this message into the polical arena as well. He delivered invocations at the inaugurations of at least two governors, a N.H. Supreme Court justice, and one U. S. senator, reminding our politicians that "all speech is babble, / all debate confused, / all proclamations null, / until the voice of the powerless / the cry for justice / the thundering protest / against violence / are heard." For the next eight years to the day, he shepherded his diocese with a firm resolve and belief that "nothing is impossible / with God."

Despite the debilitating effects of cancer, Bishop O'Neil continuted to write poetry until only days before his death, leaving an unfinished poem. One of his last efforts, "In the Hollow,"composed for the rededication of Our Lady of Fatima Church in New London, is one of his most metaphorically sophisticated, juxtaposing the changing seasons with the story of Mary's visit to children in Portugal to celebrate Our Lady of Fatima's renovations. What he says about this church serves as a parallel for his own poetic technique: "You take / all the elements / of grace and nature, / and in prayer / and sacrifice / offer them / to God." His poetic offerings brought comfort to many in religious and secular life, but what is most absent from his poetry is an imposing I. He is certainly one of the most unobtrusive of poets. Bishop O'Neil rarely wrote about himself, but in those pieces, "My Parish" and "The Soul's Triumph," he does reveal his most intimate thoughts and feelings, asking for Christ's help, "begging you to take / from me / my inner self, my limits. / The barriers to my peace, / the dyings / I cling to / block me / from resurrection..." In the end, he knew the soul's triumph rests in the crucified Christ he was looking at. He knew that his life, like his poetic voice, was a gift of God. Readers can now share in that gift.

What we know about his craft comes from his personal secretary, Helen Vollinger. The Bishop, she has related to me, worked from handwritten manuscripts which she then typed. Bishop O'Neil revised extensively, even after the occasion for which the poem was composed had passed. He did not write any of the poems in prose form and then artfully contruct them as poetry. In fact, just the opposite is true; he converted some of the poems to prose. Of the forty-nine poems included in this volume, eleven retain the Bishop's working title, designated in the Contents with an asterik*. The editor's task was to find appropriate phrases from the poems themselves for both poem titles and section headings. Information from his title pages has been included beneath the poem's title. Additionally, Bishop O'Neil cited biblical allusions in only one poem, so those have been added. Otherwise, the editing was limited to matters of stylistic consistency. As Robert F. Morneau, Auxiliary Bishop of Green Bay, says, "Bishop Leo O'Neil sang his own song, in his own way...constructed in such a way that it has its own inner melody that makes us feel life in a larger and richer sense." In his lifetime Bishop O'Neil was known as "The People's Bishop," and now we should add that he was also their poet — laureate of religious life as perhaps no other.

Ray Gamache
Assistant Professor of English
Notre Dame College

acknowledgments

I would like to convey my thanks to the following constituencies who assisted me in preparing this book:
DIOCESE OF MANCHESTER
The Most Reverend John B. McCormack, Bishop of Manchester;
Reverend Monsignor Norman Bolduc, for his kindness and graciousness as Diocesan host;
Matthew McSorley, for answering all my inquiries with considerable grace and charm.
NOTRE DAME COLLEGE
Sister Carol Descoteaux, C.S.C., president of Notre Dame College;
Dean Carolyn Hill, for believing in me from the project's inception;
Dr. Barbara A. Radtke, for documenting biblical allusions and offering insight into the poems;
Sister Cecile Charette, C.S.C., for locating sheet music and hearing the melody within these poems;
Dr. Robert E. Michael, for patiently listening to my every idea and mentoring me as only a friend can.
DIOCESE OF SPRINGFIELD
The Most Reverend Thomas Dupre, Bishop of Springfield;
Geraldine Moriarity, Edward O'Neil, (sister and brother of Bishop O'Neil), and family.

Special thanks to Helen Vollinger, who provided me with essential details that only someone directly involved in the production of the Bishop's writing could know.

Special thanks to Len Reed, who catalyzed the entire project and whose quiet enthusiasm was contagious.

Lastly, I wish to give heartfelt thanks to my spouse, Mary M. Farrell, for being my own green and orange poem, whose love makes every day an Erin melody.

I

THE STORY TELLERS

The sacrament of friendship

Priests' Retreat
Diocese of Norwich
October 1983

The obscurity
    of our origins
intensifies
    our ambiguity.

We are made
from legends
    and myths,
lured and duped
by some strange whispering
we really never fathom,
    answering
an ancient call,
"*Come and see,*" (John 1:39)
    and told
to "*go and tell*
the Good News." (Mark 16:15)

We stammer,
weighed down
    with words
that will not soar
above our own
    weariness
    and fly
like eagles
penetrating
the grandeur
    of God.

We hold a treasure
in earthen vessels,
    and
in the edge
    of sadness
that rings
    our lives
we wander on

never knowing
if our story
is heard
  or understood.

There are some
  traces of
  our origins
written by
  the struggling
  communities
stunned by the scandal
of the cross
and startled by
the surprise of
  the resurrection.

We are the
  disciples,
the chosen group
that journeyed
  with Him,
basking
in our
privileged
inner circle
  rank
until He stings
  us
with outrageous
  innocence
and demands
that we
become perfected
as His Father
and that we
  leave
all things and
  follow Him.

We are the
  boat people
  of Matthew
terrified
  in
the roar of
  storms
lost
in
the bleakness
of the fog,
until He fulfills
His promise
  to us,
"*Do not be afraid...* (Matthew 14:27)
I am with you
  always." (Matthew 28:20)

We are the
scattered
  pieces
that yearn
to be single-hearted
  so that
we can see God,
  yet
pulled
by our own
insecurities
into empty
  tombs
where He never
  can be found.

We ignite
  the fires
that become
the light of the world

for
we have known
a radiance that
shines on in darkness.

It is our joy
to magnify
the Lord,
to lay aside
all pompous masquerades
and come
before
our unpretentious God
with gifts
of bread and wine,
assembling
His people
to tell His story,
which is always
theirs
to touch their lives
with frail signs
and see
again
the compassionate
healing
of a bruised Lord.

Our God is comfortable with us
far more so
than we with Him.
Through prophets, kings,
and even rainbows,
He has made
His covenants.

But our eyes
were always dancing
for golden cities

for Him to dwell in
  apart from us
because we were
embarrassed by
  our lack
and did not understand
  the condition
for friendship
is to be incomplete.

Can you recall
those moments in your life
when you talked far into
  the night
with a friend
and you were not afraid
to share hidden things?
How beautiful
those moments are for us!
They settle deep
within our souls
and anchor us against
  the loneliness
that is us.

For from
  our lack
  our need
  our incompleteness
a friend
can touch
and release
  a strength
  a gentleness
  a courage
that lay unknown within us
and make us complete again.

Jesus, vulnerable with

all our human hurts,
met in the quiet night
to be with His friends
   before He died.

Running between
   the lines
of John's Gospel
   are all
the unsobbed sobs
   that catch
in the dread
of what is before Him
and the dark troubles
that trembled within Him.
And suddenly,
He seems to move
out beyond
that compelling design
that has always bent
His will to the Father.
From His human ache,
He sees in His need,
the father's yearning
   to be our friend
and in His own searing human pain
   knows
that this is what we have longed for
   infinitely
   eternally
to be caught in the Father's embrace.

In the anguish of leaving
He makes a sacrament
   of their friendship
and of His own will
   creates
His priesthood
that is forever.

"Behold I call you friends
for I have made known to you
all the Father has
revealed to Me." (John 15:15)

This is the gift and grace
of priesthood,
to be restless
yet so much at peace
with the deep secret of God,
to be empty
before the vast array of human need
yet filled
with the gentle power of the Christ
Who heals
and comforts,
and from our nothingness
molds a new Creation.

The priest is the storyteller,
the poet
who tells again and again
in many and varied ways
the promise,
"*Behold I am with you always.*" (Matthew 28:20)

The priest
skirts the edge of sadness,
knowing the other side
of human pain,
for he carries
in his own dust
the joy of God
and is impelled
to spendthrift
the riches of it.

We are the sign
of the New covenant,
the fidelity of God,

the means
by which He
continues to fulfill
His promise.
"*I send to you the Paraclete,*
The Consoler." (John 15:26)

For what good
are our gifts
our titles
our lives
if they do not set
the design of God
free?

What good are we
if we do not fade
and become
parables for the Kingdom?

"*Whoever loves his life will lose it*
and whoever loses his life
for My sake and the Gospel
will save it." (Mark 8:35)

We have seen
His signs
and have come
to believe
in Him,
accepted His way
and
become His disciples.

He has duped us.
His love
is like
burning fire,
imprisoned in our bones.

And He has called
us with a brother's love
by the laying on of hands
  into the intimacy
  of His friendship
that we might know
  the love of the Father
and our joy might
  be complete
and we might
  serve
so that others might have
  life
and have it more abundantly.

We are the Sacrament of Friendship!

A speck of Brilliant Red

An Encounter
At Saint Joseph's Altar
In Saint Peter's Basilica
On the Vigil of Pentecost
May 25, 1985

Shafts of sunlight
make meadows
    of art
in this ancient home
of all the nations.

Its vaulted arches
burst with gold
and vying colors
    shout
the yearning of human
    genius
to capture the glory
and grandeur
    of God.

Here always
the echo of
    prayer
    and awe
murmur like
the soft cadence of music
whiffling with
lingering incense
high up to
    the dome
that almost
    invades
heaven.

But now, as
    multitudes
of every tribe and clan
gather outside
    between the
massive colonnades,
    inside,

where the incessant
    plea of prayer
is chiseled into
walls as old
as Peter's faith,
and weary pilgrims
have worn stone
    to smoothness,
a man kneels
    alone,
hidden in
    shadows
at the altar of Saint Joseph.

It was on Saint Joseph's Day
that he was espoused
    to a people,
to an unyielding faith,
and to a relentless Gospel.
The word he pledged
on that spring day
    had been lived
and seared into his
    soul.
But now,
    shrouded
in the vastness of history,
    he kneels,
a speck of brilliant red
amid the array
    of colors
    as diverse
as human need.
He rises now
to join the others
John Paul has
called to a new
    Pentecost.

John Joseph Cardinal O'Connor
received his red hat
before the great bronze
doors of the massive
Basilica of Saint Peter
amid the cheering crowds,
but it was at
Joseph's altar
  isolated
  alone
  with mixed emotions
that he bent his
  head again
to the will of
  the Father.

For
what good are
  our gifts
  our titles
  our lives
if they do not set
the design of God
  free?
What good are we
if we do not fade
and become parables
  for the kingdom?

What good are we
if our word does not
  become flesh
  and proclaim
His kingdom?

What good is
a cardinal for
  New York
if the light

in the statue
in your harbor
doesn't beckon
him to bring
our freedoms
far out beyond
our own horizons?

New York,
New York,
you should
know, before
he went before
the great throngs,
your cardinal
    knelt alone
before Joseph,
the faithful man,
and gave his word to you again.

Resolute,
he returns again
    to you,
steadfast
and righteous
for the task.

And yet,
he must be
caught up
in the new whirlwind
that calls
    him
to be universal
for the whole church,
unwearied
in gathering
all the nations
to be enkindled

by the fire
that recreates us
and molds us
into the one family of God,
proclaiming together,
in word and deed,
Jesus is Lord.

The glory far surpassing

Three times a day
at morning, noon and night,
a melody of bells
sweeps out in silver flight
from countless towers
proclaiming "Our Lady's Hours."

To this symphony of bells
priestly hearts in unison swell.
For the bells of Mary's glad
Annunciation
tell as well
the consecration,
the ordination
of her Son.

To all the ages of the past,
they shout with hopeful note at last:
"*Cease now your sacrifice of fire and beast.*
Forever we have the priest." (Letter to the Hebrews 7:27, 21)

Spilling out against the skies,
they speak of her whose full fruition
was to bear the Life of all that lives.
Of Him they speak
the clear oblation
the perfect reparation
our eternal expiation
Christ, the priest.

Ah, we who know the beauty
of a world
abounding with the bursts of spring
can surely understand
the glory far surpassing
of her for whom these bells
so joyfully ring.

The Angelus
The Priest's Prayer
June 12, 1996

So, when the chorus of the bells
  soars in jubilation
and in surging crescendo
breaks forth in hopeful exultation,
  filling the air
with the music of her prayer
till the whole world is ringing
with the benediction of her name,
make of your hearts
the counterparts
  of these bells
and pray for us
to Christ, the priest,
that she, from
her redeeming fertility,
  will strike
within our souls
  the seeds
which fructify
and sanctify
our weakest deeds,
and that from our cold sterility
  may come
the grace
that brings forth in you
the Life of all that lives,
  Christ, the priest.

one unbroken song

Rev. Walter Pelczynski, M.I.C.
50th Anniversary of Religious Vows
August 18, 1986

Last night
was filled with
    music,
intensity,
impressions,
passions —
human and divine.

With one movement
    of the conductor's hand,
art was created and
thousands of people
    became quiet.
Only the breeze
seemed to stir.
We were pulled as
one into silent reverence.
It's amazing, isn't it,
how beauty
    awes
and holds and overwhelms us.

The chorus moved
    as one,
creating just a breath of whish
as they stood or sat
and forty or so
boy sopranos
never fidgeted.
The harmony of
    voices,
the rising mourning
    of the instruments,
the anguish of
    the soloists
as they told us
again of the agony
    of Jesus,

captivated and united us,
Gentile or Jew,
young or old.

Matthew's passion
rends the human soul.
The long mournful narrative
    enmeshes us
in the searing conflict
of the suffering Messiah,
and Bach's music
is filled with piercing
    cries.
Each
artist stood alone,
    isolated,
to take the challenge
of notes and scales
and make His human
    passion
live again in the
talent of voice.
The chorus,
knowing full well
the pain and range
of creative gifts,
sat fixed,
riveted
and consumed
in the outpouring
    of soaring
    beauty.

Jesus, in Matthew's passion,
    is bent
on doing always
the will of the Father.
It is the compelling
movement of His

life.

Halfway through
Part I of J.S. Bach's
"The Passion of Our Lord
According to Saint Matthew"
— just before
the whole chorus
stood and in thundering
waves of music
washed over us,
the narrator
moved to the center of
the stage
and filled with
power,
sang against the night air —
"The Saviour, low before His Father bending,
Would bring to pass, by His oblation,
A full salvation,
The love of God to man commending.
Prepared is He, the cup,
although it bitter be, to drink,
The which with sins of man is filled,
And overflows. He would not shrink,
But suffer all that God hath willed." (Trans. by Rev. Dr. Troutbeck)
In sharp contrast
to those words of
sorrow
is the invitation
of today's readings,
as summed up in
the psalm refrain,
"*Taste and see the goodness of the Lord.*" (Psalms 34:9)

We are pulled then
away from the bitter
aspect of death
to what the Book of

Proverbs challenges us to do
in the first reading,
"*Forsake foolishness that you*
may live: advance in
the way of understanding." (Proverbs 9:6)

Scripture speaks
  to us
about vinegar and
  gall
and every Passover must
have the bitter herbs.
But more often,
the words of the Bible
refer to land
flowing with milk
  and honey
and Jesus speaks
to us many, many times,
as He does in today's Gospel,
about the bread of life.
"*The one who feeds on this*
bread will live forever." (John 6:51)
This is the recurring theme
  of Jesus' teaching —
we will move through
  desolation,
sustained on our journey
by bread from heaven
until we come to the land
  of promise.
And in the words,
He speaks to us today,
He tells us that He Himself
  is the promise
  and the bread.
"*I myself am the living*
bread come down from heaven." (John 6:51)

Jesus, in a sense,
    is the vow of God
the promise made and lived.
There are those who
dare to imitate Him
and pledge themselves
as sign and symbol
of the covenant all of us
    made in baptism.

We come to celebrate today,
not priesthood,
    or ministry,
    or even mission.
We gather to reflect
    on that beautiful charism
of the church known as religious life.

Before we can
understand vows,
we have to understand
Jesus, the promise of the Father,
and Jesus Himself as vow fulfilled.
In swift, powerful lines,
the first book of the Bible,
    Genesis,
tells us of the triple alienation
of the human person and race.

Adam and Eve are estranged
    from God.
Long before Sinatra, they have
decided to do things
their own way.
The first human relationship
is destroyed. We have turned from God.
Cain murders Abel.
Person is pitted against
    person

and egoism breaks
interpersonal relationship.
We have turned individual
against individual.

Competition
drives people to build
a tower to see
who can reach
the heavens first.
Long before "Star Wars"
a special language was devised
so friend could understand
and stranger be excluded
within a given clan.
Community divided against
community and the third
and final alienation
took place.
We turned clan
against clan.
But God promised
and so Jesus
vowed to do His will
and the first healing
took place.
In His vowed obedience
we were liberated
and set free.
He returned us to God.

"*Greater love than this*
no one has than to lay
down his life for his friend." (John 15:13)
This totally unselfish love,
this purity of ego,
lived in celibate generosity,
the self surrender to do to the
least of humankind,

draws us back again
as family and not enemies.
He made us friends again.

"*This is My commandment:*
Love one another as I have
loved you. You will be my
disciples if you have love for
one another." (John 15:12)

"*I have not come to be served,*
but to serve." (Mark 10:45)

By teaching
and living community,
not competition,
by the poverty of his servanthood,
Jesus destroys our Babel
and sends among us
the power of the Spirit
to make us one in faith and
love, so that all of us
can proclaim to the glory
of God, Jesus is Lord.
He brought us back together as
family.

The vows
are important to us
because they are
the healing of our alienation.
Poverty, chastity, obedience
bring us to unity with
God, with other persons
in peace and charity,
and with the whole world
in the unity of the
Spirit.

Fifty years ago,
Walter Pelczynski
vowed that he would
live in imitation of Jesus.
You know the grace
and manner in which
he lived his words.
You know some of his hurts,
most of his successes.

Many of you can remember
his lonely struggles.
Many of you were his
mainstay
and his hope.

To me, his singular
gift is his unyielding
fidelity
to his Marian community.

He has lived fully
with them,
using all his energies
to build and bind
this congregation together,
willing in whatever task
he was asked to fulfill,
in total obedience
with no self interest,
the hallmark of
purity of purpose.

Everything
he did was
to herald the
words of today's liturgy,
"*Taste and see the goodness
of the Lord.*" (Psalms 34:9)

And because he had
known the bitters
of life, those words
are never pious piffle
    on his lips.

He has met the
cross of defeat
    and rejection.
He has even known
the anguish of physically
dying and returning
to accept God's will to live.

It was fitting
that this celebration
of his fifty years
    began
on August 15,
    quietly, with
his Marian brothers.
And it was more than
    symbolic
that his community
began this public
    celebration
at Tanglewood last night.

Music has
much mission
about it.
Every vocalist, every
instrumentalist,
must give eyes fixed
    on the conductor,
must be totally absorbed
in the mystery of the moment.
And every religious

must be totally possessed
by the mystery of Christ,
submissive to the will
of the Father.

But the conductor
does not exist
for himself;
he lives to exalt
the talent of others.
His power pulls
from them the best
    of their gifts.
The conductor must
possess poverty
of ego to let the
music dominate him.
He only is its servant.

Orchestra and chorus
are harmonies
devoid of competition,
blending community
    of gifts to form
transcendent beauty
that purifies individual
gifts and molds them
into one glorious unity.
Father Walter's
vowed life has
been one unbroken
    song,
sung to the glory
    of the Father.

The Eloquent Force

The Catholic Transcript
December 5, 1986

Shame on you,
  Bishop Hackett!
What right do you
  have
to become
what your name
  signifies?

We'd all be a
  little bit more
  comfortable
if you were a
reed shaken by
  winds
instead of
  a steadfast
shepherd, leading
  your people
by your cross
  into their own
resurrections.

And look
  at your clothes!
Why can't you
  be content
with soft garments?
Why do you plod
  along
arrayed in meekness,
tolerance and kindness?

Whoever
  said you
had to prophetically
  fulfill
the name your
parents blessed you

with
and become John,
beloved of God?

Why do you insist
on echoing for us
in your life
the enduring love
of the Father
making even the
mumble of your word
soar us into
intimacy with
Him?

Why do you
bother us
with your
simplicity
that eloquently
forces
all of us to
be what we
should become —
Christian?

Why can't you
parade around
with a little
bit more pomp?
Your unpretentiousness
is a bother,
always reminding us,
of what good are
our gifts
our talents
our lives
our titles
if they do not

set the design
  of God free.
What good are
  we
bishops, priests, sisters,
  people,
if we do not fade
  and become
parables for the
  kingdom?
Oh, why didn't your
  parents
give you another
  name?
For then we could have
just looked for an
  ordinary prophet.

Why did they have
  to pick John?
We would have been
  satisfied with a
  light that does not
shine on in darkness.
And why did you have
  to become by
the way you live your
  life
not just a herald
but good news
joyously lived?

Bishop John Hackett,
  shame on you!
You make us all
  become authentic.
So, hang in there,
for our sakes!

A Joyous Burden

Father Tom Curran
60th Anniversary of Ordination
May 25, 1980

Sixty years a priest.
Sixty years of living
and revealing
the secret
that the Lord Jesus
spoke to His priests
the night before He died.

For when He gathered them
at that first Eucharist
He said to them,
"I call you friends."
And like us when we are among
friends
He went on to share
His deepest,
most intimate thoughts.
The secret he revealed
to them
was God's tremendous love
for His people.

The Gospel of today
is part of
that conversation
Jesus had with
His first priests
and His prayer to the Father
for them.
"*...these men have known*
that You sent Me;
to them I have revealed
your name
and I will continue to reveal it
so that Your love for Me
may live in them
and I may live in them."

(John 17:25-26)

This is the secret
Jesus whispers
to everyone He calls
with a brother's love
to be a priest,
and seals it
as Jeremiah the prophet says
"*like a fire burning*
in their hearts
and imprisons it
in their bones." (Jeremiah 20:9)
That fire will never be
quenched
until it has empowered
other hearts
to be blazed
with the love of God.

This is the grace and gift
of priesthood,
to be restless
and yet so much at peace,
to be empty
before the vast array of need
and yet filled
with the gentle power of the Christ,
who heals
and comforts
and from our nothingness
molds a new Creation.

The priest is the storyteller,
the poet
who tells again and again
in many and varied ways
the promise
"*I will not leave you orphans...*" (Lamentations 5:3)
"*I am with you until the end of time.*" (Matthew 28:20)

And so for sixty years
this poet priest
has told the story
of how much God loves His People.
As news of this celebration
began to make its
way through parishes
in which he served
memories were stirred
and stories told again.
Several who knew him
over thirty springs ago
said of this gentle priest,
"He didn't save himself
in his dealing with the sick and elderly."
They remember him walking
to their homes
because he had given up driving
and didn't want
to impose on anyone else.

"He didn't save himself
and he was so consoling."
A woman of eighty years now
recalls him
and speaks of him
being with her family
when her mother died.
What a blessed recollection
to have of someone
after all those years,
to hold someone in quiet memory
a priest who was "so consoling"
when there were deep hurts to be healed.

As stories were recounted,
I'm told,
many of his friends were amazed
that they all had in common

one strong and powerful
recollection of him.
They were startled that in the midst
of fond memories
they remember a special pain of his.
If there was a rift
in any family
and sisters and brothers
would not speak to each other
he would carry it as his own
personal burden
and agonize until he could reconcile them.

He was a priest for families;
his devotion to his brother
and six sisters
made him that way.
Father Curran preached for
worked for
suffered for
and carried the burden for family unity.
It was the singular gift of his priesthood.

The deep, quiet calm
of this priest
led this parish
through the tumultuous
changes
of the sixties,
never forcing
but always guiding
his people
in liturgical renewal
and insuring
that all was done
with a deep love
and loyalty to the Church.

For sixty years

the joy of priesthood
has been his.
In my conversations with priests
who were his associates
these past several weeks
I've heard them speak fondly
of a man they describe
as thoughtful,
and sensitive,
as kind,
not overbearing
or demanding.
They say he was a friend.

Seated at table
with His priests
the Lord Jesus,
my dear people, prayed also for you.
"*I pray not only for them*
but for those who will believe
in Me through them." (John 17:20)

It is the joyous burden of
the priesthood,
to stand before the Lord
and beseech Him on your behalf.

For sixty years
in Word
in Sacrament
in prayer
as healer
reconciler
listener
friend
Father Curran
petitioned
God for you.
Remember the story

told long ago
of Moses praying for his people
on the mountain
with hands uplifted to the Lord.
While he prayed
the Israelites prevailed in battle
but when in weariness
he dropped his suppliant hands
the battle turned against them.
And so the people
sent up to Moses
two men to hold up his tired arms
and soon the victory
belonged to Israel.

Sometimes I am so deeply moved
when I see how our priests,
and I, myself,
besieged with so many tasks
are sustained by our good people.
We are truly partners;
we cannot endure without each.
We are confirmed in each other's strengths.
I am grateful
for all that you have done for Father Curran
for our priests and for me.
It is a source of great joy
to me
to know
that this good priest
is here in his beloved Berkshires,
but it is a special consolation
to know
that his home is in
this particular rectory
with his pastor who was once his altar boy.
For if we did not have
words like
thoughtful, kind, wise,

gentle, we would never
be able to describe Msgr. Paul Riedl.
His associates
are good and sincere priests.
I am happy that Father Curran is here
because this is a priestly house
and that's the only home he deserves,
the only place he could be happy in.

Sixty years ago
the great churchman
Cardinal Gibbons
ordained to the priesthood
Father Thomas Curran,
friend of presidents
and missionaries,
pastor and poet,
who tells us that his
porch is now his parish.
"Now that I can't walk.
It's simple, not garish,
but there we can talk...
there's a roof up above
and a wide open door
and the people I love
come to me as of yore.
I no longer preach,
my approach is a smile
that always can reach
the people worthwhile.
My choir's but one chord
I have little to give
but it's all for the Lord
for as long as I live."

My God, grant Father Tom
many years of preaching
from his porch
in his beloved Berkshires.

until the end

Henry Smith
Ordination to the Diaconate
December 31, 1982

There is more
than one ending.
Even the
wish of sympathy
is varied
in tempo or motif.
Novelists
and playwrights
anguish
with creator's
pain,
holding taut
suspense until
the end.

You call
us here
to end
a year
with Mary.
This young
and gentle girl
walked
hills much
like ours
and heard
a thousand prophecies
cry from
every brook
she leapt
across.

Every meadow
and all the
valleys
spoke of her fullness,
yet she
walked alone

and terrified.
No one
noticed that
the dream of God
was dancing
in her eyes.
She stood on Judean
hills
and ended all of
Israel's dreary
yearning —
the surging longing
that swept
from century to century
and spoke from urgent
desolation
of Messiah, Emmanuel,
the Desired
of the Nations.

She spoke,
"*Be it done,*" (Luke 1:38)
and Isaiah's,
and Jeremiah's,
and Elijah's,
and Micah's,
and Moses',
and David's,
and Solomon's,
and God's
unfilled desire
was ended,
"*And the Word*
became flesh." (John 1:14)

Deacon Henry,
end the longing
of those who
dream

in empty isolation
for a kingdom
which does not
   exclude them.
Walk like
   Mary
in hospital corridors,
   in soup kitchens,
through poor and
   tired streets.
Let the exiled
see the dream
of God dancing
in your eyes,
and let them
   know
the tender God
   you are ordained
   to serve.

Deacon Henry,
   you bring
   us here
on December 31,
not just to end,
for that is hardly
   Mary's song,
nor life,
nor consent,
nor vow.
You call us
   to see you
   become filled
with her expectation,
restless
with her zeal
to make your whole
   being proclaim
the greatness of the Lord.

Deacon Henry,
  like her,
you wait
for the fullness
  of time,
and in that solitude,
your soul magnifies
  the Lord.
The hungry will be
  ministered to,
the lowly will be
  noticed,
for you have sworn
  as the covenant He
made to Isaac
  and Jacob
  and all the fathers,
that you will be
  no more
  no less
than she
who was the servant
  of the Lord.

And so, all ages,
young and old,
will call you
  blessed,
because, like her,
you surrender
  everything at
  His word,
and forever will
  echo her,
"*My whole being*
  proclaims
the greatness of
  the Lord." (Luke 1:46)

remembered wisdom

Father Edward T. Fitzgerald
25th Anniversary
June 3, 1984

There comes a
point in the
Hebrew scriptures
when memory
becomes reality.
The remembered
becomes so powerful
it lives.

Jesus, as He walked
with the two disciples
on the road to Emmaus,
recalled the scriptures
so vividly
that those who accompanied
Him
later said, "*Were not our*
hearts burning within us?" (Luke 24:32)

It is interesting
to note that one of the
two disciples
on the road to Emmaus
was probably a woman.
One is named
Cleophas. But in
St. John's account
of the passion,
Mary, wife of Cleophas,
is standing beneath
the cross with Mary,
the Mother of Jesus, and
Mary Magdalen.
That adds a powerful
insight into the Emmaus
story, a married couple
on a journey, trying
to comfort and

console one another,
bewildered and
crushed because
things did not turn
out the way they
thought they would
   or should.

The priest is
   the storyteller,
the memory maker.
The whole reason for
his existence
is a short, one-liner,
"*Do this in memory of Me.*" (Luke 22:19)
Without those words,
we have no mandate,
   no Eucharist
   no community
   no people
   no priest
   no existence.
Even in the most
primitive cultures
memories are collected
   as histories.

We do not live
   without a story.
In Africa, encamped
around leaping fires,
a chieftain molds
   a legend
   to stand against
the roar of animals,
prowling in
   the night.

In Ireland,

as gray mists
swirl in lowery
clouds,
the storyteller
gathers in a
cozy pub
to weave with lilting
grace
a myth
out of such a simple
and ordinary thing
as a bird
with a broken
wing.

And we have
seen the shadows
of tree limbs
moving across
bedroom walls,
heard the creak
of stairs
listening to a
scary bedtime
story,
always prepared
for a quick dive
under the covers.

There are
those who tell stories
with dramatic flair,
exciting enthusiasm,
wild imagination,
dashing romance.
Surely, Father Ed Fitzgerald
is not among them.
Flair, exciting,
dashing romance

are adjectives that
ding readily off
his head
or are reserved
by him for a golf ball.
But he is
preeminently the storyteller
because the priest
is chosen not to
tell his story
but Jesus'.
He is not to confuse
or usurp,
to burden
with words,
to interfere,
to get in the way of
the message.
He is simple,
told to make
the memory live
with no clutter,
no pretense,
to let the power
of the Word
take flesh in his
own life
so that it
confronts and
comforts others.

Sometimes
the only way
to tell a story
is to listen,
to walk the
journey
with the confused
and downcast

and allow
their words to surface
and reveal
the hidden mysteries
of their lives.

Father Fitz
learned to be a
good listener
on the street corners
of Holyoke.
When you're the
shortest guy in
the gang,
you have to do a lot
of listening.
He also learned
how to tell the story
on Brown Avenue.
When I think
of compassion
or gentleness,
I often remember
a woman with the
bluest eyes I've ever
seen.
They brimmed with
laughter,
frowned with concern,
embraced you with
care.
Nora Fitzgerald
was a regal
woman
who long ago
taught me
that dignity is
often born in poverty,
and respect

does not come from
accumulated titles
    or arrogance
but from the
    quiet resolve
to know your own
goodness and live it.

In 1983, I had the
privilege of preaching
about the Quiet Men of Holyoke.
Those who knew them
can easily recognize
Michael Fitzgerald, Senior,
    in lines like these.
We who have grown up
    in this city
have known the quiet
    men
those self-contained
    reserved
    emotionless
    unmoved
    unyielding men
whose strength would
stay off our affection
or shrug away our
    concern.
Born to fish in clear
    streams
and walk through
    hedged fields,
these men were poets
    and dreamers,
visionaries and scholars,
    who worked with
the stench of rag
    and pulp.
Can you recall

meeting the men
of the older generation,
walking up the hill
with them?
They were bone tired
from a day working
in the mill,
but they always
treated you with
respect.
They always
called you
by your first name,
and they made
you feel important.

Much of the story
we tell
is remembered wisdom —
the faith lived
out for us
not as taught by
theologians
but by people
who were so
totally consumed
by the Gospel
they hardly knew it.
It was their lifestyle.
The clerical
heroes of Father Fitz
were never cardinals
or bishops.
They were priests
entirely different
from one another —
one, a pastor
whose antenna
could readily seek

out the hurting
in every corner
of the parish;
the other, a
curate with
uncommon gifts
who was always
trying to fade into
the background.
Fitz could have
become "churchy"
long ago,
but the walk
from Brown Avenue
to Northampton Street
had too many pitfalls
on the way,
like street corners
and ball fields.
Baseball averages
were more important
than who was transferred
where
and clerical gossip
infinitely boring
compared to the
antics of the
characters at Schmitter's.

Abraham is the first
believer.
Without giving
any guarantees
or even offering
any incentives,
God speaks to him
and asks him
to set out on a
journey

without a destination.

Each of us
does the same.
Few of us
who answer a
call to serve
    the Church as
religious or priests
ever thought
things would
turn out the
way they did.

If we even had
a clue to what
    it would be like,
we would
have headed for
    Tahiti years ago.
And few of you
who opted for
matrimonial bliss
would ever have imagined
things would be the
    way they are.
    The journey,
whatever turns it
takes, is made
bearable by God's grace,
and, in most cases,
that grace is evident
in the people who
walk the journey
    with us.

There are some who shout
directions with military
precision who think they

are easing your burdens,
but they give nothing
except a severe headache.
There are some who
are so sympathetic
that they never
give you the joy
of occasionally
feeling sorry for
yourself.
There are the
Dear Abby's, the
pied pipers, the
thundering preachers.
And then there are
those who quietly
walk along with
you — chuckling
occasionally,
swinging imaginary
golf clubs in the midst
of your distress.
They are the ones
who silently enter
the journey of a
couple on the way to
Emmaus, whose dream
has been shattered —
and after they've gone,
we realize they told
us the whole story.
People like
them are apt
to give up
a comfortable parish
assignment and
go off to the confusion
of Vietnam because
they understand

street corner theology —
that presence can take
away a lot of fear.
And people
like that have
deep personal
    friendships.
And people like
that don't need
words to tell
    the story.
We are all
    storytellers.
But the power of our
    story
lies in how close
it comes to that
    of Jesus'.
Every line written
    about Him
    is about
    us.

The greatest thing
any priest can do
is to make memory
become so vivid
    it becomes real.

Father Fitz is
    a great priest
because there is
    no adjective
that fits him more
than one powerful
    word.

He's real.

The perfect sacrifice

Prayer for Priestly Vocations
April 7, 1997

Jesus,
Light of the World,
send us priests
to illuminate
the darkness
around us
with the radiance
of your Gospel.

Jesus,
the Way,
give us priests
to walk
with us
on our pilgrimage
of faith.

Jesus,
the Truth,
grant us
priests
to lead us
deeper into the
mystery
of your faithful
love for us.

Jesus,
the Life of the World,
inspire
in the hearts
of young men
a desire
to offer
in your name
the perfect
sacrifice
for the salvation

    of the world.

Jesus,
the Healer,
we need
priests to pardon
us by your power,
to strengthen us
in your grace
and lift us up
    in hope.

Jesus,
who ministered
to the poor,
mold priests
to your image
that we may be a
    Church concerned
for the homeless
    the powerless
    and the voiceless.

To you who
live with the
Father and Holy Spirit
be praise
    and glory
forever and ever. Amen.

II

From These Back Porches

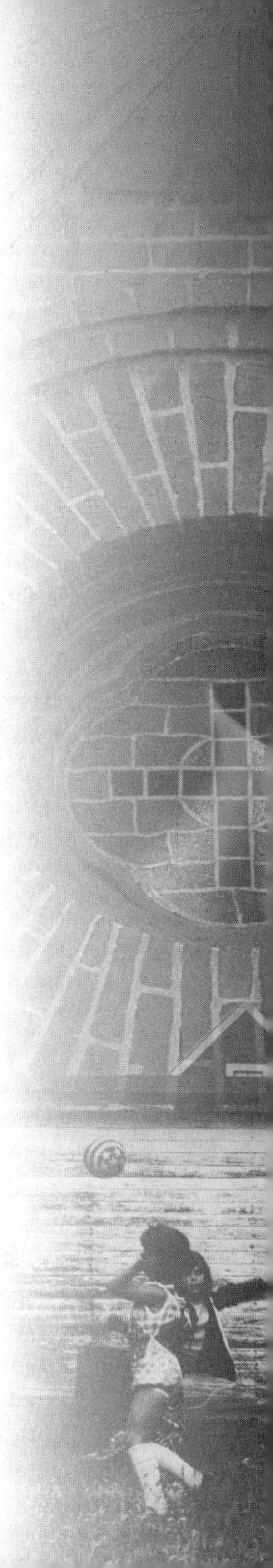

The Quiet Men of Holyoke

Homily
St. Jerome's Church
March 19, 1983

Of all the
plaintive songs
our language knows,
the burdened
words
of a grief-driven father
are the most haunting.

The troubles come
again
to Ireland
and the strong,
strapping lad
who broke
his back
every day
with him in the
fields,
eking from
the desolate
land,
a poor living,
is called
by mournful pipes
to march to war.

The weary father
climbs the hill
and
watches his son
until his back
is just a speck
in the soft Erin evening.
And then,
all his unsobbed sobs
and
unspoken words
mingle in the shroud

of Irish mist.
"Oh Danny Boy, 'tis you,
'tis you
must go
and I must bide." (Fred E. Weatherly, "Danny Boy")

The wrenching pain of
Ireland
is
held captive in these
words,
but their real beauty
is the whispering touch
of music
which,
once for all,
breaks Irish silence
and flings
across hills
and
valleys
an oft hid story
of a father's fierce love
for his son.

For there have
always
been the
sad leavings
in Ireland,
her young,
barely out of
teens,
torn from home
and sent
to battle
or exile,
far from cottage
and hearth.

And the pain
    of parting
always lingered
in their eyes,
as well as the yearning
to know
    again
the music
and the storytelling,
and the fiddling
that dances a village.
And the laughter of youth
that was never theirs.

We who have
grown up in this
    city
have known the quiet men,
those self-contained
    reserved
    emotionless
    unmoved
    unyielding men
whose strength
would stay off
our affection
or shrug away
our concern.

They worked the mills,
built the great dam,
flung against the skies
our lofty churches.
Born to fish in clear
    streams
    and walk
through hedged fields,
they were poets

and dreamers,
visionaries and scholars,
who worked with the stench
of rag
and pulp
in paper mills,
or had their lungs
clogged with
irritants of
textile fibers.

In the Gospel of today,
Jesus
is speaking
in a village
when suddenly
a group of self-righteous
men
push a woman
through
the crowd,
and in one of the most
embarrassing lines
of Scripture
John says,
"*They made her stand there*
before everyone." (John 8:3)
Jesus, the quiet man,
was so angry
at their humiliating
accusations
He stooped
and played
tic-tac-toe
in the dusty road
until He could
check His anger
and then, straightening up,
He glared

at these pious frauds
and challenged
them with unflinching
stare,
"*He who is without sin,*
let him cast the first stone." (John 8:7)
And then,
with sheer disdain,
He went back
to tracing
in the dirt.
When all had gone,
He gently helped
the woman
to her feet
and asked her,
"*Is there no one*
to accuse you?" (John 8:10)
"*No one, Lord,*" she said.
And in reply
He said,
"*Nor do I.*" (John 8:11)
And beyond forgiveness,
He gave her back
her dignity.

That's a special
grace,
to give dignity to
another person.

What I remember best
about Holyoke
is that older generation
of quiet men
who gave us
manly dignity,
the understanding
priest who,

after you had
confessed all your
teen-aged confusion,
would whisper,
"Pray for me..."
and made you think
"I can't be so bad
if he needs my prayers."

Can you recall
meeting the men
of the older generation
and walking up
the hill
with them?
They were bone-tired
from a day
working in the mill
or in the city yard,
but they always
treated you
with respect.

Remember sitting
on a sparkling
September afternoon
at McKenzie Stadium
watching
the Knights of Columbus tournament.
How proud you felt
when one of these
men of the older generation
would ask you
what you
thought of a play
or an umpire's call!

They always called you
by your first name,

and they made you
feel important.

Kids did a lot
    of business with adults
in those days
    because they ran the
errands...on foot
to the grocer
    the tailor
    the drug store
to buy the fish and chips
and if there was
any money left over,
    to pay the bills.
That older generation,
    bearing the scars of origin,
waited on us
as though we were
    their equals.
They treated us
    with respect.

Those quiet men
who preceded
our generation
loved this city.
They recognized
the geographical
    beauty
of its boundaries,
a city
almost
built on a
    mountain,
sweeping
down to
and ringed
by the

river,
terraced by
canals,
speckled with
parks
and ball fields.

There is in the Gospels
another story
that reminds me
of these quiet men,
the parable of
the restless youth
who demanded
all his inheritance
and having received it,
slammed doors
and stomped through
fields
searching for his
freedom
in far-off places.
His anxious father
went
to the top
of the hill
every day
waiting and watching
for a familiar figure
to appear.
(How many parents today
sit by phones
and jump at
the first ring
hoping for the return
of a child they love?)

We call
the biblical searcher

the Father of the
Prodigal Son.
And the day he
recognizes
the figure hesitantly
approaching
on the path,
runs to gather servants,
clapping his hands
for attention and shouting
orders, "Kill the fatted calf,
hire the band,
invite the guests,
pour the wine.
My son is home!"

There is no less love
in the father of
Danny Boy.
How many times during
the day
would he go to the post
hoping for a letter,
or drop the hoe, scan
and search the distance
until one day
far, far off,
he picks out
a tiny dot
approaching
and knows it is the
stride and gait
of his boy.
There is no shouting
or hand clapping
or hurrying
to the cottage.
There is just the
quiet pretense

that everything is normal
until he goes
to the house
for tea,
throws his
hat on the peg
and says to
the wife,
"Put down another cup.
The lad is on the road."

And when the young man
enters the house,
there is no hug,
    only the greeting,
"Is it yourself that's home?"
For the forever burden
    of the Irishman
is the silence
    of his love.

Those men of Holyoke
could spellbind
you with stories
and charm with
eloquence,
but they hardly
ever said,
"I love you.
I'm proud of you."
Their language
was a deeper
    clearer thing.
Words could be
wasted on
    politics and
    sports,
but the deep pull
    of affection

left them silent.
We know
their haunts,
Dingle, Hampden,
Springdale, Kerry-Pulaski Park,
and a few
more obscure
places
for a game of not
so quiet cards.

You'd see them
slip into the chapel
right next door
or find them sitting
in the back row
of almost every parish
church.

They were their own
judges
and often
measured
themselves
too harshly against the Gospel,
but they struggled
to live
its word.

They too would
react
with scorn
against
the blathering
of gossip,
and a sharp
"Be still"
would cut off its source.

How often
did we
hear
them say,
"They have enough
   troubles
as do we all.
Let them be."
They would make
   outcasts of no one.
They had endured
   its misery too long.

They would
   respect the poor.
It was once
   their title.

These silent men
would speak out
   against injustice.
It was their
   history.

And they would
   rejoice
in a Pope
who took on
   the whole world.

You
who will
set out
tomorrow
to parade through
Holyoke
are the
   sons
   and grandsons

of that
strong,
quiet
generation.

Your march
through their
  streets
is memorial to them.
They loved this city.
Build it again
  in their honor.

Tonight and tomorrow
Holyoke
honors
  a man
who embodies
in his personality
all the traits
of the men of Holyoke
  who are
our once and ever
  heroes.

From the Valley Arena,
  to crowded basketball courts,
  to McKenzie Stadium,
Holyoke has always
  cheered
the athlete of
  easy grace,
whose skill
requires no subterfuge,
the classic
  player
whose respect for
  others' art
marks him

a fair and honest
    competitor.
He is the pro
who can pull
    talent
from others
and mold
    them into team.

And Holyoke
    has always
    admired
the "quiet man,"
who, confident
    of who and
    what he was,
was never afraid
to make friends
    with anyone,
    even the outcast,
and was never
    concerned
    about power
because he
always knew
honors and position
are hollow things
and the only real
    leader
is a servant.

So, when
the whistle
    blows
tomorrow
and the drums
    roll,
Holyoke will
march behind

a man (Bishop Joseph Maguire)
who prides
himself
in one title only,
"*I am Joseph, your brother.*" (Genesis 45:4)

And yet, for us,
he is more.

He is sign and symbol
of a father
searching and
seeking reconciliation
with all who are hurting.

He is the quiet man
whose love for us
is silent
and sure.
He is the priest
whose happy task
is to
always give us forgiveness
with dignity,
and whose proud
burden
is to ensure that everyone,
even the least,
possesses it.

And he is the truly
human man
whose deepest hurt
is to be rejected
as friend.

When we
see him wave
along the way tomorrow,

we will be reminded
of a long litany
of men of character
  and nobility
and we will almost hear
  their cheers,
for in Joseph, our
brother and friend,
they would find
all that was
  good and decent
  in them.
And they would give
him their highest praise,
"He is a giant of a man."

For it is our
  shepherd's
  ministry
  to remind us
that "*the pipes*
  the pipes
  are calling
from glen to glen
  and down the
  mountainside." ("Danny Boy")

And now, 'tis we,
  'tis we must go,
not off to war
  or exile
but to speak out
  in Gospel tradition
given to us
  by them,
those quiet men,
against appalling
  oppression
or arrogant

defiance
of human right
or hope.

So, "*when*
the summer's
in the meadow,
or when the valley's
hushed and white
with snow," ("Danny Boy")
in every season,
not just St. Patrick's
Day
it is
our Bishop's
sacred pledge
to be sure
that come we back
to those steadfast men
to their faith
to their memories
their challenge
their dream.

And it is the pride
of Joseph,
our brother and friend,
to let us know
in the quiet
echo
of their silence,
it is not just they,
it is our God
Who says,
"*I love you so.*" ("Danny Boy")

Daniel
the accent
of that name
is filled
with simplicity,
void of
all pretensions.
It embraces you
with utter candor
and shatters
all defenses.

Daniel
rings the cry
of prophets,
reminding us
we have no
lasting city,
challenging us
to fight
whatever lurking lions
trouble us.

Daniel
is the fearless prophet
who dares our courage.

Daniel
lurking
in the music
of that name
are the
lilting pipes
of Ireland
and
the story of
a grieving
father's love

and

unrelenting

cadence

Daniel Doyle
September 24,1982

for his son
told in a
song too
beautiful
to be sad
but haunting
        us
with wrenching
        awareness
that every greeting
is tinged
        with farewell
until our
yearning prayer,
"*O come ye back*
in sunshine or in shadow," (all ref. to "Danny Boy")
is stilled
in heaven's quiet.

Danny
the melody
of that name
is filled
with manly grace
like
a runner
lithe and lean
enduring
bursting
against
the limits
        of time,
pushing to be
        free
and streaming
trails of
        glory behind.

Danny
mixes in its
beat
the little boy
and
the man.
It echoes
shy smiles
that lead
you to be
trapped
unaware
in friendship
and hide-go-seek
shyness
that fades in
among
the crowd
but all the
more
stands out
because
loyalty
cannot be hid
or goodness
or unabashed
sincerity.

Danny
cannot be said
without music
without an insistent
determined and
unrelenting cadence
that captures
in its Gaelic
stubbornness
the steadfast
will

    to be
    simply
        me
    and to be free
    of molds
    or styles
    or any superficiality.
For all the seasons' songs
    of Danny
    we must return
to words
sadly whispered
to the back
of a young lad
    leaving
to fight in Ireland's
terrible troubles,
"*'Tis you, 'tis you*
    must go."
For bravery is
    a two-edged sword.
"'Tis you must go,"
    commands
proud courage.
But what pain
    and what piercing bravery
is wrenched in that next
    line —
"*'Tis you must go*
    and I must bide."

"And I must bide."
What hurt
    in the remaining!
What loneliness
    in the vigil!
To Danny's friends,
    his brother,
    his sisters,

to Jenny,
  to those strong,
  silent, kind,
young men
who came
to stand beside him again,
to his mother and father,
to all of us who mourn,
the song too beautiful
  to be sad
will give us
the unashamed
opportunity to say,
"*O Danny Boy, I love you so.*"
For Danny,
  as St. Paul reminds us,
has fought
the fight. He has finished
the battle. He has won
the race
and merited the crown that
  awaits him.
The runner is filled
  with manly grace.
That shy smile will never fade
  nor its friendships die.
His goodness
has been found out.
He streaks
across the finish line,
the cheers
  ringing in his ears.

He is home.
He is free.

TO the Arch of sky

Alan Hendry
August 8, 1984

Alan was a forester
  a designer
  protector
  conserver
  of woods
  and trails
of tiny, fragile
  flowers
catching
flittering
sunlight
through tall
and stately trees.

And he never
  missed a beat
of the lyrics
  hummed
in his forest.

There once was a
  day
when all the
  grandeur
of what he was
and what he loved
was swept up
  from the floors
of his meadows
  and woods
to the arch of sky
  above.
Family and friends,
picnic arranged,
  sat in the fields
  and the silence
  of the forest
was broken again

by the Word of
God.

This is my Body.
This, my Blood.
And Alan, who knew
that all creation was
holy,
saw and knew that
it was good,
and he was extremely
glad.

Alan,
the music
of your life
drew its strength
from the stillness
of love
flowing deeply
within you.

And it was fitting
your final legacy
to Nancy,
the counterpoint
of all your harmony,
was the melody
of a song
winging its way
up through the
trees
to eternity.

In a Quieter Way

Doctor Frank Mills
1983

Of all
the charisms
possessed by
    Jesus,
healing
was the gift
He delighted
    in.
He spendthrifted
    it
as He went
about His
    ministry
through Galilee
and all Judea.

His other gifts
    were not
without the shadow
of personal pain.
He preached
as one having
    authority.
It was a gentle
    message
and liberated
    the outcast
    and the poor,
but it imprisoned
    Him.

He was a sensitive
    prophet
Who saw
    chaos can
    be turned
    into cosmos
only by the

ordering of
unselfish love.
But denial
of vested interest
is not easy
and those
who proclaim it
are often
branded trouble makers
and revolutionaries.
Maybe healing was
the Lord Jesus'
only consolation.
Even when people
    simply touched
the hem of His cloak,
He seemed
    to know
both the
yearning need
and the unseen power.

Sometimes
those He cured
jumped up and down
    with joy.
Sometimes
they stood dazed
    in awe,
speechless at
    such a grace.
Sometimes
they were silent,
    pulled
into the deep
    mystery of
God's surging
    power,
the raw, creative force

of the energy
of love
grafted into the
marrow of their being.
And sometimes,
as we all
know,
they did not
even say,
"thank you,"
or let the
grateful moment
touch their soul.

In the strange
paradox
of what we are,
we have so many
other comforts
in family
in friends
in pleasure.
But once
we move
beyond
that enraptured
spontaneous kiss
that makes a
little child's
hurts
"all better,"
we find to our
stunned surprise
that when we heal
others
we ourselves are
often wrenched with pain.

Maybe

that's because
we live
in fuzzy vision
of life dimension
and we do not
have the scope
of God.
And maybe
that's why
Luke,
who is called
a physician,
describes Jesus
as the infinite
healer
Who can
make the lame
skip and dance.

Who empowers
the sightless
to see
the entrancing,
whimsical beauty of
the rainbow.
Who makes
the deaf hear
the cooling
rush of water.
Who stoops,
and with a simple touch,
brings profound peace
to troubled minds
and tortured souls.
But our healing
is finite
and fragmented,
and it is often
our brokenness

and our pain
that ease
suffering
and make others
whole.

What doctor
is not terrified
at failure
or not numbed
in the frustration
of his own helplessness?
What pressure
on the mind
when questions baffle,
doubts lurk,
options evaporate,
and time, far too little,
disappears like
grains of sand.

The healing
profession
is difficult
not so much
because
it involves
our human woes,
but because
it pushes up against
the Creator's turf.

We can handle
the human complaints!
The demand for perfection
is tough on our nerves
and often strains
family life,
but it can be endured

if one is hard-nosed
and stubborn enough.
But, like
   Jacob,
we shy away
from wrestling
   with God.

There comes
   a time
in every healer's
   life
when that moment
cannot be postponed
when the shattered,
   broken,
weary, gifted,
learned, pressured,
anxious technician
is confronted
and arm-wrestled,
drawn into conflict,
tired, tested,
until the indispensable
gift of the healer
is meshed in his soul.

Certain
   people
become
   their name.
They grow
into it unnoticed
until one day
it dawns on us
that this name
   expresses
all they are.

Frank
a name without pretense,
without any subterfuge,
    direct
    to the point
    brittle
    honest
    blunt
    confident
    self-assured
    steadfast.

Frank
    the name sums up
    the man
and gives direction
    to his life.
The name
moves beyond
    the man
into the mystery
of who and what
    he was.

Frank
    a man who zeroes
    in on issues
    impatient with trivia
    or circuitous paths
        to truth
        to friendship
        to professionalism.

A man becomes
    a surgeon
through skill
    training
    experience
and dogged determination.

He becomes
  a healer
in a quieter
  way,
drawn to demanding
  compassion
through his own
journey of brokenness
  lonely
  frightened
  frustrated
supported by family
  and friends
but always standing
  alone.
Confronted by the
vast array of human need,
  helpless
at his own inadequacy,
he is born from
  overwhelming
  insecurity,
but confident in his own
  gift.

With deft hands,
he probes pain,
isolates it,
cuts through it.
He learns
all the subtleties
  of what we are,
the mysterious
  thread
of elements that
go beyond the
  fading
beat of pulse

and make him
revere the
life we are.

All of us who
  knew Frank
know that he was
  his name.

And all who
  met Frank
know that somewhere
  on his journey
he became
what he wanted to be.
Beyond
  physician
  surgeon
he was a healer.
And because
  he was
  a healer,
he was beloved
  as husband,
honored
  as father,
trusted
  as friend,
revered
  as surgeon.

He was quite
  simply

Frank.

The surer path

Geroge Frost
March 13, 1985

There are liberators
who call crusades,
gather clans
and armies,
march and conquer
enemies,
and then become
the oppressors.

There are others
who take the
surer path
that breaks bondage
and sets
people free forever.
They have no power
but
they empower.
They dictate only
with wisdom.
They never
control or confine.
They challenge
to broader scopes.
They push to the limit,
but not for personal gain;
their conquest
is to let the human
soul
know its
own talent
and infinite worth.

They are the poets
the dreamers
the seekers
and teachers
of truth,

who splash
our world
with beauty,
energize it with
  imagination,
ennoble it
  with dignity.

When does
  the dreamer
become determined?

When does
  fantasy
conquer reality?

When does
  a man
walking these streets
begin to know
that he has
  been woven
from the weariness
  of these mills,
from the back breaking
  walk up these hills,
from sharpened
  wit and
  wisdom
of unschooled scholars
  whose
sure clarity
make him
itch for knowledge?

George Frost
  was molded
from the richness
  of this city —

its playgrounds
   and people
its mills and mountains,
its river and woods,
   and its greatest
   treasure —
its poverty.

George Frost
   understood
that the
undergirding
   of Holyoke
was a rare bonding
of old neighborhoods
and honorable ancestors,
of varied cultures
that once joined
would be invincible.

It probably
startled him
that he became
the adhesive force
that rallied people
   silently
   quickly
into an uprising.

The incessant
   drumbeat
of that revolution,
gathering momentum
   and building
into an exciting
   crescendo,
was the recurring
   melody,
"Give everyone a chance."

Then suddenly it
   happened!
The dreamer was determined.
Fantasy became a reality.
The man, woven from
   the firm fiber of this city,
became the scholar
making others scratch for
   knowledge.
And then,
gates of ghettos
   and
imprisoning mills
   were flung open
   and steps
quickened down
   stairs
and criss
   crossing
paths led to
   a building
   where a
Teddy Bear
of a man
   changed
the center of Holyoke
to the corners
   of Beech
   and Sargeant Streets.

I suppose
that seems a
   bit
   dramatic,
but for thousands
   of people
who told their
   own stories

these past few weeks,
every time George Frost's
name was mentioned,
it became again very real.

This tall, lumbering man
  has taken
the best of what we
love in this city
and built it into
  a dream.
The Community College
is not his memorial,
the city of Holyoke is,
as it is to all of us
who loved growing up here.
The real memorial
  of George Frost
is that he was a
  liberator
who set people's
  minds free
  from their poverty,
who ignited their
  imagination,
and who left
  their destiny
  right where it
  belonged.
And in that, he
  gave all of us
as his final challenge:
Ennoble every
  person.
Bless them with
  dignity.
Give them a chance,
for that makes us
  all liberators,

but make them
understand the rest
    is up to them.

That keeps us from being
    oppressors
and makes us
    the poets
    the dreamers
    the seekers
    and teachers of truth,
splashing our world
    with art and beauty,
energizing it with
    imagination
and ennobling
    with dignity.

George Frost did that!

The singular, silent beauty

Mrs. Annina DiGiulio
October 26, 1987

There are some things
that are
so spectacular
you can't ignore them,
a blazing sunset
or a blaring band.
Others
lure us
because they are silently
singular,
a tree in a meadow,
unnoticed at first,
surrounded by such radiant
autumn colors
that suddenly
you are startled
into understanding
that this
is the thing
that sets off all the others
and pulls them together again.
Or out of nowhere
a note in a song
lifts out of
the melody
and shatters beauty
into your soul.
It has such
clarity and purity;
it is so
rapturously true
that you are
stunned by
the surprise of it.
Your soul
becomes lost
in the sound of it.

Butler Court
explodes with energy
    and intensity.
Music blasts, cars roar,
exuberance and moods
swing in radical
    arcs.
But thousands
of college students,
    preoccupied with
swirling worries and fears,
in the midst
of their own confusion
    linger
over the sight
of a tiny woman
    and her dog,
sitting on her porch
in the warmth
    of the sun,
smiling at them
passing by.

How many times
have most of you
    walked into
a crowded room
dinned with conversation
and felt yourself
    magnetized
to the spot
where Annie sat,
her fingers moving,
    soothing what she held,
    restlessly searching
for a nurturing thing
to do for you?
Did you ever notice
how her hands

seemed always
to be fingering
   rosary beads
no matter what she
   was doing?
There are some women
who, no matter how
elegantly dressed
   they are,
look as though they
are wearing aprons,
waiting for a chance
to sit you down
   and serve.
And aren't aprons
   really
what St. Paul meant
when he said, "You
have been clothed in Christ Jesus"?
Aren't aprons,
after all, our baptismal robes?

Annie DiGiulio
was the singular,
   silent
thing of beauty,
the graced moment,
the lilting note
that soars above
   the melody
   and sears
us into the
core of God.
For anyone who ever
looked into the mirth
of her eyes
saw the dream of
God dancing
   there.

with trills of tenderness

Gail — Your name has the whisperings
of angel wings
that sweep across frozen fields,
making them leap
to life with spring.
Like Gabriel,
who stands among us and says,
"*Rejoice — O highly favored —*
the Lord is with you," (Luke 1:28)
you brim with life
and bring us
to the joy of God.
His sun is dancing
in the golden tangle
of your hair;
His mirth is caught
in the merriment
of your eyes.

Gail — You swirl around us
like the wind
and hold us
in the vortex
of your memory,
storming through us
your zest
your charm
your lilting grace.

Gail — The music of your name
soars up
beyond our tired pain
to search and to speak up
of a shepherd's tenderness
who stoops to free
a lonely lamb
and holding it close

Gail Smiaroski
November 1979

sings a happy song
to ease its fears
and with a steady, confident hand
heals its hurts.

Gail — The music of your life
is in the melody
of a name that rushes
with trills of tenderness
to scoop all in joyful embrace.
Let your laughter
ring in our ears,
your lovely sparkle
pierce our pain.

Gail — Pert and pretty
lure us past
the anguish of today
to that one eternal moment
when there is no more hurt,
or pain, or tears,
when the world
of the past
is gone
and all things are new
when we shall be together
merrily in heaven forever.

# of so soft a Loveliness

Kelly Christman Nadolski
Memorial Service
May 26, 1986

Last week
clouds and rain
shrouded us
and sealed
chilled sorrow
  into
the marrow
of our souls.

We need to remember
the brighter days
  of this spring.
Did you notice
this year lilacs were
more beautiful,
more abundant?
Even if they were
  far away,
in distant meadows,
you could feel
  their presence,
their scent stirring
  in the breeze.

They came before the heavy rains
  could burden them.
They glistened only in morning dews
  and danced dry
  in the sun.

Lilacs
are enduring,
strong, disciplined to the art
of resisting buffeting winds.
And yet,
there is a hidden shyness
  and frailness
  about them.

They seem so overwhelmed
 by our admiration
that they quickly
hide and disappear.

Kelly was like
 lilacs of this
 spring.
You could feel her aura
 long before you knew her.
Like a riptide of energy,
 she seized beauty
and spun whirlpools
of words and images
 that sprung
 in frenzied dance
into our souls.
She splashed
lines and shadows
 that pulled
us into deeper
 meanings.

She pierced
the mystery of life
and persons
 so deep
she was afraid
she had trod on
 private ground
and would withdraw
 back into the
shell of her own anguish
 afraid her eyes
would reveal too much
 of us
 to us.

Her pain

was not so much
she could not bear her own,
and as it was
she could not
keep ours
from hurting us.
Her promise is
not ended.
It lives in
every dance,
in every lilting song,
in every tear
that trembles out of fear,
in every boldness
that has the courage
to see the depths of beauty
and never run from its angst.

Her gladness lives
in every trill of laughter,
in paintings
that astonish us,
of revealed realities
obscured by our superficialities,
in sharpened words
that challenge art
to move beyond entertainment
and seek its own perfection.

The brighter days
of spring have
now returned.
The greens
are deep and loyal.
Show-off clouds
pirouette
in endless stages
of blue skies.
Birds

chirp a chant
that eases mourning.
Flowers
timidly brush against
    our focus
like puppy dogs
trying to comfort
    our brokenness.

This day
of so soft a loveliness
    is Kelly,
shyly tugging at the sleeves
    of ourselves,
pleading, insisting,
"This is really
'my kind of day.'
This is what I sought
    relentlessly —
so much awesome
    beauty
    gentleness
and sheer delight.
Forget all my other days
    for this bright
    and glorious
    day
is mine forever."

The other side of joy

Mary Boyle
February 21, 1985

The Gospel of Emmaus
is not usually read
at funerals.

It was chosen by
Mary Boyle's sons
because it was their
mother's favorite gospel.

From what I know of
Mary Boyle, it was also
the gospel she lived.

Some scholars
say that the two disciples
described in Luke's
account of this resurrection story
might have been
husband and wife.

St. John, in his account of Jesus' passion,
records that near the cross
stood His mother and His mother's sister,
Mary, the wife of Cleophas.
I find that interpretation
especially beautiful,
for part of every marriage
is described in the Emmaus journey.
Two people, filled
with love, tenderness
and hope, set out
together.

The power of their
affection holds
them, but
disappointment
disillusionment

discouragement
shatter dreams
and make
them, as Luke says,
downcast.

Then, as they begin
the lively exchange
of going over and
over these sad
events,
an unknown
presence joins
them.
"*He asked them, 'What
are you discussing as you walk
along?' They stopped,
looking downcast...And then
He began to explain
and interpret
all these things
for them.*" (Luke 24:17, 27)

That
unknown presence
we all know is
the God of love.

It startles me
so many times
when I discover
the God of love
quietly weaving,
intermingling, revealing,
binding, in our human loves.
Haven't you discovered
moments in your
deepest friendship
when your ideas became

one,
when you felt infinite
depths within you,
when, without words,
you spoke and listened
and love — God — was
revealed?

Was this why
Mary Boyle loved
this Gospel?
Did she know
the divine intrusion
that explained
the unexplicable?
Had she so intensely
loved
husband and family
that she brushed against
the quiet eternity of God
and found Him the
tranquil companion of
the journey that so
often for her was
filled with hurts that
could not be prayed
away?

I am pleased that
Mary Boyle's sons
have chosen this Gospel
because it made me
reread John's
account of the passion
and discover again
that beneath the
cross stood Mary, the wife
of Cleophas.
Because this woman,

whose journey we
come to celebrate today,
stood, always
    steadfastly,
    courageously,
by the cross.
For rooted in
    faith,
she knew
that all these
    things must
    be endured
and that
    once embraced,
the cross sets
    us free
    to glory
in our own
new creation.
For our pain
is the other side of
    joy;
our hurt, the
binding of reconciliation;
our loneliness,
the longing for the
unending moment of love;
our death,
the fullness of life.

The Emmaus Gospel
has some of the most
memorable lines of the scriptures:
"*Lord, stay with us. It is growing late...*
while he was with them at table,
he took bread, said the blessing, broke it,
and gave it to them. With that their eyes
were opened and they recognized him,
but he vanished from their sight. Then

they said to each other,
'Were not our hearts
burning within us...'" (Luke 24:29-32)

I hope these words
live in Mary Boyle's sons'
lives.
How many times will
you recall the tender
look on her face?
How many times will
her strength touch
you?
How many times
will your heart burn within
you when you experience
again the depth and
power of her love
for you?
Our God is so simple
with us.
He sits at table and
chats and shares
His life and love.

No wonder Mary Boyle
loved this Gospel.
Recall the jokes, the
chatter, the family
feuds and forgiving
at the kitchen table
and know you came
to recognize love
in the breaking of
the bread.

No wonder
she
understood the Eucharist!

Like any loving mother,
she was of its substance.

"*Stay with us. It is getting late*"
    is your final prayer,
but, if you are her sons,
only by letting her vanish
from your
    sight
will you know that
she indeed has been
    raised up
and lives forever.

"*Mane nobiscum.*"
"Stay with us"
is her promise
fulfilled to you.

from These Back porches

St. Patrick's Day Mass
Holyoke, Massachusetts
March 22, 1980

St. Patrick's Day
is a time for memories,
  a time
for remembering a city
  as it was.

Tonight for just
a few moments,
I would like
to call forth
  again
from these
old and tired streets
  the memory
of a group
  of people
whose lives
are part
of the history and destiny
  of this city.
Tonight I would like
to reflect with you
  on the
Women of Holyoke.

Forty years ago,
long before we heard
  the expression
"the inner city,"
these apartment blocks
  were bulging
with families
  held together
through a terrible depression
by the sheer determination
  of wives and mothers
who would not be daunted.
They withstood

the closing
of one mill after another,
kept their families together
and gave us a
legacy of faith
and trust in the Lord.

It's amazing how much they saw
from these back porches.
Any infraction of the
family code of behavior
would be dealt
with swiftly.
What escaped
their notice
they were certain
would be dealt with
on Saturday afternoons
in the parish confessional.
And peace reigned
in the neighborhood!

Can you imagine
the endurance of these
women
who, as young girls,
went to work
in the textile
or paper mills
and who,
after hours of drudgery,
would wearily walk
back up these hills
keeping a wit,
a laughter,
and a gentleness
that belied
the harshness of their lives?

I have been among you
    long enough
to know the story of these women
and to have heard
you mention also
the great women who
built the public school system
    of this city.
Their names are
    legend now.
They shared zeal for learning,
pride in ethnic cultures,
and motivated their students
    to achieve success
    through education
and service to community.

Holyoke
is also blessed
    with families
whose strength
    is found
    in sisters
whose sacrifice
    sent brothers
on to college
    to be doctors,
lawyers, teachers and priests,
    or who
stayed behind
to take care of
an elderly mother or father,
    or who,
in some cases,
raised a brother's
    or sister's
children.
They became the favorite
    aunt

and we probably
will never see
their like again.

But in recording
  the history of
the women of Holyoke,
we cannot forget
our women religious,
  for from here
the Sisters of Providence
  began
a health care and
social service ministry
  that still
remains unparalleled
in western Massachusetts.

And here, the Sisters of St. Joseph
  together with French
  and Polish communities
began a school system
which continues
  to shape
the lives of Holyoke's citizens.

To these congregations
  went hundreds of
Holyoke girls
who distinguished themselves
as caring, compassionate
  signs of the Church.
Our women religious
  have become
national leaders
and have contributed
greatly to the renewal
of the American Sisterhoods
and the Church

in the United States.
The accomplishments
of the women of Holyoke
   should give hope
to the Hispanic woman
who confronts poverty
   and a new culture —
in a sense,
almost lost
in a lonely exile.

The women of Holyoke,
   graced with the
beauty of young Colleen,
steeled with a spirit
   born of faith,
blessed with a wisdom
   taken from the
land of saints and scholars,
give the only
   gift
that can break the
harshness of a mill city —
their gentle, untiring, enduring love.
In the midst of all
   our celebrations
it is right that we should
   honor
The Women of Holyoke.

III

Emmaus Roads

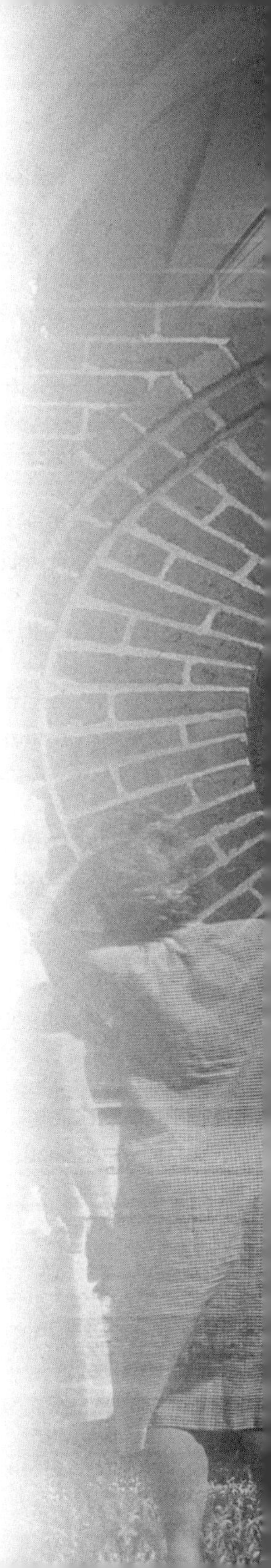

into unending springs

Sister Katherine Hinga, S.S.J.
Final Vows
June 6, 1981

All of us
have
walked
Emmaus roads
where
scorching suns
relentlessly
caked
our weariness
and
dusty trees
reflected
our
wilted spirits.

Emmaus' road
is cluttered
with dead illusions,
and desert
winds
brittle
their
chill
into our
shattered hopes.

Who
of us
would
have dared
risk
Easter joy
to join
these two
whose
anger
and
resentment

mingled
with the
scuffs of
dust
like the puffs
of broken
dreams
of all our human pain
made
more bitter
because "*we*
were hoping
He was the One." (all ref. to Luke 24:13-35)

"*Why*
are you
so downcast?"
heard
in the
emptiness
of a fading
afternoon
is spoken
still
as classrooms
empty
to students
too young
to be
without hope
and in
tenements
to people
too old
to be alone.

How slow
we are to
believe.

We pay
no heed
to prophets
who say to us
war no more.
War never again.
We marshal
weapons
and armies
and we do not
listen to the message
of Calcutta
or hear
the anguish of
El Salvador.

But He
Who
rises
above all death
began
to
explain
to them
and to
us.

Emmaus
is lived
always in progress
in conversation
walking
together
always forward.

The past
is just an
interpretation
of our

roots
planted deep
only
to enable us
to break
forth
into unending springs.

You
are
not like
the woman
who was
Lot's
wife.
You do not
look
back
upon
destruction
to
be petrified
by the past
and fixed
in
salted
terror
by
future
insecurities.

Have you
ever
heard
of a
woman religious
who
wanted to return
to the past,

or whose
burning
ambition
is still
to keep all the pins
that she might find?

A
vocation
fired
in the
excitement
of the
sixties
must live
out
the Emmaus Gospel.

There was
a
call
then
to bold frontiers
by a young
man
who saw great visions
and
to open
windows
by an old
man
who dared
to dream
new dreams.

And
suddenly
they
were gone

and cities
and
campuses
and human
hearts
were downcast.
We were
hoping
that this was
the time
and our
anguish
was bitter.

In our strange
call
who can tell
when
Jesus approaches?
Or when
the explanation
begins to
make
some sense
and our hearts
burn within us
and
we begin
to understand?

At what
point
in our
return
to
our roots
are
the seeds of
simplicity

and justice
sown
and,
like Jeremiah
says,
imprisoned
in our
bones?

When is it
that the Spirit
has the final
say
and we *will* to
use
our freedom
in joyful
service
to a whole world?

And why
is it
that when
we do
as Jesus did
and from the
beginning examine
our roots
we are not led
back
but forward
to find a
whole new way?

And stand
surprised
that from
all our churning
and all our deliberations

through all
our doubts
and insecurities
we are called
as ministers of the
   church
gathered together
on a Sunday
   morning
   in
   March
and called
   to
go beyond
   justice
and even
   charity
to use our celibacy
   and ourselves
to make of
   the
stranger
our dear neighbor?

Maybe
it is when
we recognize
Him in the
   broken
   bread
and we know
   that we
   like Him
are only free
   when we serve.
Then He vanished
   from
   their sight
and then

they return
back
but now to the
new creation
whose only constitution
is as John says
to love
one another.

For some
that strange
decade
of the sixties
will never end.

There was
too much challenge
too much hope
too much excitement
to ever let it go.

Deep in some
are its anguish
its hurt
its dream
and its cry for justice
and human dignity.

For some
these will always burn
within their hearts.
For them
we pray the Emmaus
words
etched on this tabernacle
"*Mane Nobiscum, Domine.*" (Luke 24:29)
"*Lord, remain with us.*"

Kathy —

only the
fear
the doubts
the bitterness
and the resentment
of Emmaus ended.
But all the rest of the
journey goes on.

He still asks, but now through
you —
"*Why are you so downcast?*"

He still explains the prophets
but now in your witness.

He still makes hearts burn
for justice but with you.

He still remains with us
through your vowed ministry.

He still is recognized in your brokenness
that others might be made whole.

He still is Easter joy in your community
which makes of strangers dear neighbors.

waters of clarity

Humanitarian Award of the
Nashua Charitable Trust
Sister Jeanne Perreault, P.M.
May 14, 1997

Her academic,
    civic
and religious community
involvement
are quantitatively
and qualitatively
close to infinity.

She is a woman
whose presence
commands respect.
Tall and graceful,
when she enters
a roomful of people,
she is noticed.
Not, surely not,
because of her high
fashion.
Not, certainly not,
because she bubbles
with chatter.
She draws people
    because
she is serene.
She is a woman
vortexed
in a buzz
of activity
but at its
    center
her personality
is dominated
    by silence.

She beams
the startling
    message
that good works

are passing crusades
and trendy causes
unless they are rooted
    in prayer.

She has a virtue
whose name I
do not know.
But it is a habit
of profound thought
    a stance
    a way of being.
In the wellspring
of her soul
    is a
churning
against the currents
of holding on
    and the
freedom of
letting go of selfishness
so that the
    waters of clarity
and lucidity
can reach purification
in the crystal
    splendor
of ideas splashing
against
eternal truths
and granite reality.

And thus
she wins trust:
no masquerade,
no pretense,
no playing games.
She stands
among us

as a woman
who delights
in being
our sister.
And that
is what she is —
beyond teacher,
civic leader,
and even faithful
  religious,
  she is
Sister.

And she is not afraid
to risk
all that name involves:
  bonding
  enduring fidelity
  confidentiality
  forgiveness
  steadfast loyalty
  honest confrontation
  astonishing affection.

Jeanne
always wanted
to be a sister.
In the honor
bestowed on her today
  you confirm
that her dream
has become
a reality,
for you
name her
  your
faithful
  Sister.

from Relentless suns

Sister Mary Scannel, S.S.J.
25rh Anniversary
July 17, 1983

Prayer
is sometimes
as brittle
as grouchy kids,
riding in hot traffic,
coming home
from the beach
with too much
salt and sand
   and sun,
touchy and
whining,
till fresh,
cool waters
have made
them civil
   again.

The psalms
   of vespers
sung on
July afternoons
are like that —
droning on
   and on,
hanging limp
and heavy,
weighed down
with burdens
of unfulfilled
   sighs
of Israel.

Then, all of a
   sudden,
there is a youthful
   stirring,
emerging from

ancient chants.
Like a sudden
rush of breeze,
a new beat
swings against
ancient melodies.
"Magnificat anima mea" (Luke 1:46)
"My soul proclaims the greatness of God"
dances across
  history
and ripples
new hope
to tired prayer.

Prophetic oracles
have met the moment
and promises are
forever kept.
A young girl
named Mary,
poised against
the centuries,
sings her song.
It soars
against Judean
  hills
and like incense,
  whiffs
in mystic prayer,
the surging
  joy
of one who has seen
the greatness
  of the Lord.

But, this woman
is not content
to speak of
pledges now fulfilled.

She wraps herself
in prophetic
   cloak
and usurps
the charism of Moses and Elijah,
Isaiah, Jeremiah,
Micah and Osee,
and all the heralds
   of Yahweh's
revealing word,
   and stands
the first of all
   the prophets
of the Word made flesh,
   and proclaims
the new order.

"*His mercy is from*
   age to age.
He has routed
   the proud of heart.
He has pulled down the mighty
   from their thrones,
   exalted the lowly.
The hungry He has
filled with
   good things
and the rich
sent empty away." (Luke 1:50-53)

Then,
the melody
   fades.
And yet,
its startling
   challenge
hovers,
   haunting
   and

taunting
souls
restless
with the energy
of God.
Mary is
no cool-cheeked
madonna.
The arms that
lift jars of water
are tanned from
relentless suns.
Shadowed in
her eyes
is the pain
of rejection
and accusation
which almost branded her
as one who broke
the law.
Her yes to the
mysterious lure
of her vocation
to be the handmaid
for all the human family
left her destitute
against
the wrenching
plan of God
that demanded
not comprehension,
but
unflinching
faith.

This is our God's
most gentle gift
to us.
For, her struggle

her pain,
and her terrible confusion
are our journey
and our story.
We are so used
to guarded yeses
that her trusting
shatters us
into compliance.
We are a driven
people.
We cannot be
in love
and live without
faith.
It is the one condition
that love demands.
It insists
that we leave
all known boundaries
and walk where
there are no certainties.
The future is not
conditioned on
our plan.
It is merely accepted
without reservation,
not to subject
us to its whim,
but to set us
free
to do the will
of the One we love.

Isn't that what
marriage is really
all about,
to hold all tomorrows
in the spectrum

of unselfish love
that risks everything
   in faith?
And isn't that
   the promise
of every Christian
   to take time
   and make it
the history of Christ?

We are all Jacobs.
We feel unworthy
that somehow
we have stolen
the birthright
and prerogative
   of another
and are embarrassed
   by titles and
identities and names
that mark us holy.

We all find ourselves
   wrestling,
not with some dark evil,
but with a strange
force of goodness
that is surprisingly
   within us,
constantly
calling us to
a greatness beyond
   ourselves.
Like Jacob,
we limp along,
knowing our weakness,
fully aware
we have stolen
our brother's clothes,

because, after all,
we have been robed
    in Christ Jesus.

Like Jacob,
we demand
to know
the name of
this aggressor
who arm-
    wrestles
us to the ground
and like Jacob,
whose request
went unanswered,
we find
in the struggle
during the lonely
    night
our own identity
as he was
named Israel.
In the anguish
    of every
death and resurrection
    moment
that churns
within our souls,
we know
    our name
is Christian.
It is the web
    of the Gospel
that tangles
us in its trap.

There is not elite
    among us.
Every one of us

must confront
   ourselves
with the Gospel
or we will never
find comfort.
Acceptance of
the lingering
   illness
of a husband
is witness
   of a wife's
   and mother's
   faith that
never yields.
And disappointments
   that rend
   us hopeless
give testimony
to the strength
of our determination
   to live
the good news
in season
   and out.

It is only
in the poverty
of our incarnating it
that the Word
   becomes flesh.
And so the
faith of the
Mary who
comes here
   today
to make
the Magnificat
her song
is rooted

to the springs
  of fidelity
planted in her
by mother,
father,
brother, sister
and sustained
by a community
  of women
who watched
the design of
  God
take startling
  twists
and bring
  an
  unassuming
elementary school teacher
from her classroom
to dusty roads
in Thailand
  and from
  quiet gifts
that loved to
create liturgies
  and sit
in the inscape
  of music
and be at peace
  with God
to mold
a new compassion
  in her
born in the
energy of listening
and burnt
in the Jacob
struggle
searching for

unquestioned
identity.

Mary,
  may
the Magnificat
  speed
you on to the
  mission
and ministry
you are called
  to be.
Remind us
of the compassionate
mercy of God
Who tumbles
  the proud
hangs around with
  the lowly
and Who can
  make
  grouchy kids
on a hot July afternoon
sing with
  the delight
of a double-scooped
ice cream
  cone.
For God
  is joy
and He has
done great
things for you
and through you
has enriched the poor
and troubled
and fed them with good
  things.
Holy is His name!

In Suspended Harmony

Sister Jane Morrissey, S.S.J.
Silver Jubilee
October 15, 1988

The grandeur of God
  is splashed
all around us
on our autumn hills.
This week, awesome
  dawn
and evening skies
unraveled,
telling us,
"The piercing
  presence
of the Holy
  is here."

And now,
a woman
  gathers
family, friends,
bonded sisters,
and Church
  to celebrate
and in the midst
of fidgeting children —
  saludos se hablan
in Espanol (la lingua,
  de Dios) —
singing processions,
a venerable mother
  offering gifts,
joy becomes an
almost tangible beauty,
an experienced reality.

But all of us,
once upon a time,
have walked upon
a hidden
  loveliness.

Alone in a forest
a shaft of light
hits upon
  a flower
  a bird
  a doe
and we stand, stilled
  in reverence.

Or we enter a
hospital room
  or a prison cell
  or a barrio shack
and look upon a face
  and see
  a soul
and we're stunned
because we
  know
the Transfiguration.

Isaiah's
  words
  today
are brittle
and harsh
but when they
  are broken
they shatter
  our souls
with the victimization
  of God.
And leave us
spellbound,
awed
by the deepest mystery,
  the ultimate,
  infinite beauty.

God is a suffering
   servant.

The design of
   the Creator
spendthrifts our
imagination —
   pond grass
   purple flowers
   a baby's little fist
tingle us with delight.
But how could we
   ever grasp
the unpretentiousness
of the dynamic
love-impelled
   energy
   of God
whose Christ
through His suffering
   justifies many
and bears their guilt?

Have you
ever borne
the guilt of another?
When someone
   you cherish
hurts you
and they don't
   know it?
A woman bearing
the guilt of
her husband's
broken fidelity.
Or nations like
Haiti enduring
the guilt of betrayal
   by leaders,

the Church
absolving the most
arrogant of sinners.

No wonder
the quiet rapture
of Paul's words,
"*We do not have a high*
priest who is unable to
sympathize with our
weaknesses," (Letter to the Hebrews 4:15)
lays hold
to the core of hope
in each of us.

Long ago,
we were
taught
that a fundamental
ingredient
of beauty
is symmetry —
all things
held together
in suspended
harmony.

The symmetry
of God
is relational
and always leads
to intimacy.
For
God is person;
more,
God is love.

The essence of love
is to share

to be bonded
to serve.

In the gospel
Mark
describes
the symmetry
that God demands
of us.

Jesus has just
shared
the pain
the apprehension
the dread
the intimacy
of His approaching death
with
His disciples.

He has hardly
finished
when He is asked about
who will sit
at His right
or His left in the kingdom.

Have you ever
shared your deepest
thoughts and fears
and when you've finished
heard
the person
to whom you've
revealed
these deep troubles
respond,
"Do you think
the Red Sox

will make it next year?"
Then you understand
the vulnerability of God.

Discipleship
can be reduced from intimacy
to trivia.

We can
ritualize
pompize
theologize
politicize
our intimacy with God
because we are
afraid to
accept
the symmetry
of the Cross.

What strange
compelling beauty
in that person
who comes
to serve
and not
to be served!

Jane,
your soul
has always
sought
beauty
in words
in art
in idyllic ideas
and philosophers'
whims.

And yet
there were quiet
rivers running
in you
that always
knew
the hidden
loveliness
in the human soul.

And you dare
to be disciple
to seek the
intimacy of God
and bear the
pain of it.
To walk in
the contrasts
of shadow
and light
of human joy
and hurt
that constitutes
the beauty
of person.

To dream
to have the courage
to accept
a Suffering Servant
as a God
demands
we live in ivory towers
and be somewhat
naive.

It pulls us to
mysticism
and the spaced-out

dimensions of life.

But it is
the only reality
the only wisdom
the only strategy
for peace.

For twenty-five years
you have been
a disciple
never afraid of the
intimacy of God
or servitude
to our exiled
alienations.

And so you
have been

Teacher of Peace.

come bursting in

Sister Alice Bovat, S.P.
Twenty-fifth Anniversary
April 17, 1982

It's surprising
that the evangelists
give
Mary Magdalene
a
title
and even
more surprising
that
we never use it.

She is the Disciple
of the Resurrection.

It was not Mary
sinless
and model for our
faith —

Nor was it Peter
the blundering
builder of the Church —

Nor John
whose intimate love
of the Lord
bound into the apostolic
tradition
soaring insights
into
God's yearning
for His people.

It was Mary
Magdalene
who ran
breathless
through the cobbled

streets of
Jerusalem
in that
bleak
dawn
that held
so much of
our hope
in its mist.

It was
this woman
who, liberated
by love
from all our slaveries,
became the first herald
and
the real image
of the
New Creation.

It was she
who in a
sense
called
together
the first
council of
the Church
and she who
announced
its first dogma
"*He has been raised...*" (Mark 16:6)
and she
the first to witness
to it
and to testify
to it....
"*I have seen the Lord.*" (John 20:18)

In the perplexities
   of our
vocation
we need to
   be reminded
that *she* is the
Disciple of the Resurrection,
   for she
more than any
   other
   tells us
   who we are
and maybe
   that is why
she was chosen.

We cannot
   be Church
nor community
   vowed
   committed
   or pledged
until we are
   disciples.
And there
   is
no other
   title or
designation
that has more
   meaning
or authority
or validity
than that.

It was the Lord Jesus
Himself
who schooled her.

She heard His words,
saw His scorn
for self-righteousness,
knew His compassion,
sat spellbound
as He spoke of
His "Abba..."
who, like a parent
who had lost
a child,
would scan
  the hills
each day
hoping to
catch in the
distant specks
  a gait
that love would recognize.

She was there
  when He comforted
  the poor
and when he
  confronted
  their oppressors.

Each word she heard,
each gesture
  of friendship
  of forgiving
  of healing
was release
  for her
and an enabling
  that called
  her forth
  from
  rank tombs

and empowered
her to "love much."

For this is
discipleship —
to recognize
our own emptiness
and to
be set
free
from prisons
and to
know the
paradox —
whoever loves
life
will lose it
and whoever hates it
for My sake
dances in a thousand
eternities.

Magdalene
is made
of sturdier
stuff
than sword
slashing
heroes
who run
in the darkness
of the night.

She climbs
the hill of Calvary
and learns
what it means
to be disciple.

She wades through
  defeat
and the terrible
  aloneness
that shouts
  across
brooding fields,
"What's the use?"
So much
for pious practices
unending self-denials
and cumbersome
  obediences.

Devastated
she still follows
even to the tomb.

How often
  we are
reminded,
especially
by Paul,
that the cross
  is necessary
for Resurrection.

We can
  echo
His cry for
  justice,
show compassion
  for His poor,
forgive
  and
heal in His name.

But first,
like the Magdalene

we must
let His love
  set us
  free
from our vested
self-interest.
We must
  be one in Him
and
  not escape
  His cross.

For twenty-five years
you have been
  disciples.
You've done
a thousand
good and generous
  things.
You have been
tested and tempted
by the tensions
  of renewal
and community.

You have been
  weary
  and anxious
confused and questioning.

So many times
  it seems
like the ninth
  hour
when darkness
  covers
the whole earth
and we feel
our cry should

be, "*Why*
have You forsaken
  us?" (Matthew 27:46)

But the three of you
  come here today
to say to us,
"*Why are you*
  so slow of heart?
Did you not know
that all these things
must be done" (Luke 24:25-26)
in order to have
all things fulfilled?
You say to us,
"*Were not our*
hearts burning
within us?" (Luke 24:32)
You come
on this day
of spring rains
washing away
memories of
depressing April blizzards
and speak to us
of the vision
of fields filled
with flowers
and freshening springs.

We live
in hope
because
you are
Disciples
of the Resurrection
and you
come bursting
in

upon us
with balloons
with new promise.
Be for us
  forever
Disciples of the
  Resurrection.
Constantly call
  us
to go beyond
fads and trends
  to faith —
to faith
  that trusts
in spring.
"*Unless the grain*
  of wheat
falls into the earth
  it remains
  just that.
But if it dies, it
  produces much." (John 12:24)

Sadly
the Gospel
tells us,
"*the men put*
  no faith
in Magdalene's
  words." (Luke 24:11)
It was ever thus!
She showed 'em!
It will ever be thus!
As a community, and as individuals,
it is your responsibility
to imitate her
and be Disciples
of the Resurrection.

That maddening gleam

Trant, Sister Regina Mary, S.S.J.
Liturgy of Christian Burial
Wednesday, January 11, 1989

Regina,
you scandalized us!
When you fluttered
into a room,
you went chirping
  along,
beguiling us
with flirtatious
twinkles in your eyes,
  enticing us
to be a bit reckless,
  to live it up
and be believers.
We had become
so sophisticated
  in our theologies
but with a flip
  of the wrist
  you waved,
like a beaded purse
holding a flapper's treasure,
  your rosary at us.

After you had listened
  to learned lectures,
could we detect
a defiant flounce
in the bob of your wig
  as you opened
your tattered formulary
and went back to your
  essentials?
Some people
are too light for heavy
  lifting.
You were a feather.
If you didn't
wear a winter cape

to hold you down,
a good winter wind
would blow you away.
But you did
the long haul.
You quarterbacked
   the whole game,
threaded the needle time
   after time,
threw more than your
share of Hail Mary passes,
even ran through
   tough blockers
and never got
caught behind
the scrimmage
   line.

Bruised and battered,
worn out and weary,
you hung in there.
But that maddening gleam
   in your eye
always made us wonder
   if you
knew something we didn't.
You frustrated us.
In the midst of all your hurts,
   how were you so sure
He was always there?

You had no right
   to be as joyous as you were.
One look at you
and we'd hear
   the pealing,
soaring, triumph
of bells, bursting
in an ever spring

air —
"Regina Coeli, Laetare. Alleluia."
"Rejoice, Queen of Heaven. Alleluia."

No regal stance for you.
No Elizabethan, nor Victorian
regina for you.
You followed the peasant girl.
Generations from
age to age
will proclaim your generosity,
for your whole being
was present
to God your Saviour.
You never ruled;
you served
and earned the kingdom.
How many keys did you punch?
Columns did you add?
Envelopes did you record?
How many lessons of
business decorum?
How many rosaries
did you say for us?
And, Mother of the Maccabees,
did you ever stop
saying aspirations?
How are they ever
going to hold you down?
We always suspected
the dancing shoes were close by.
With bangles and bubbles
and bows,
you'll rock the place alive.

Regina,
ring the bells.
Set loose
a thousand

crashing choruses.
As you parade along,
hear the shouts
of your cheering fans,
the saints
you have been hounding
all these years.
They're giving you
a standing ovation
and all along your
path, they're
shouting,
"Laetare, Regina, Laetare!"
And she, whose lines
you're stealing,
is beaming.
She recognizes
another whose motto was,
"*Be it done to me*
according
to Your word." (Luke 1:38)
And she adds
the final rallying call,
"Laetare, Regina, Laetare."
And we, too,
can be at peace.
Now you know
that the God you loved
so totally
so completely
loves you even more
than you do Him.
And for all the ever
eternities
you understand
how deeply
we cherished you.

Regina, laetare. Alleluia!

WOMEN OF PROVIDENCE

Sisters of Providence
Chapter
July 3, 1981

The Word of
God
comes
to us
today
first through
Joel,
who tells
us
the spirit
will be poured
out
and prophecies
and dreams
and visions
will work
wonders
in
the heavens
and
on the earth.

As you remembered
last
week
did you get
again
the courage
to dream
like
that first band
that
came to Holyoke's
poor?
These resolute
women
would
not brook

within themselves
fear
or tiredness
incompetency
or aching
loneliness
for home.

There are women
who care
for a brother's
or sister's
child
or stay behind
to nurse
an aging parent.
Such a task
demands
denial
and emptying.
We can
imagine
then
at what
costs
they became
Sister
to homeless
and aged,
healers to sick,
and
comforters
to the betrayed.

What sighs
of weariness
mingled
with prayer
at Farren

Providence
St. Luke's, St. Vincent's
Mercy.
What was the pain
of Brightside,
the hurt of the Guild.
Long before
books were
written
sociologies
studied
or techniques formulated,
they
had to be
the answers.
You've heard
again
this week
the stories
of these
noble women.

Someone
among
you
said
she would
have rejoiced
to see
new challenges
you face
    today
as you dream
    your
new dreams.
I suppose
as old
stories
were being

told,
you remembered
how you
yearned
for
some free
time
so you could
have
the delightful
pleasure
of starching
your garniture.

There were
those of us
who
thought
it was an
architectural wonder —
curled flaps
or flat ones
notwithstanding.

And so now
    it is your
turn.
Others worn
and weary
kept the dream
    alive.
Now, not fully
comprehending,
they say
to you,
"Don't be afraid...
go on."

And so with

the power
of their
prayer
we come
to hear St. Paul
remind
us —
we boast of our
hope.
The new poverty
of your
vowed
life
is insecurity.
Each one of you
has talents
needed by the
professional
world.
Among you
are some of
the finest
administrators,
counselors,
technicians.

In the state
your gifts
would command
huge salaries
and give
you much fame
yet
you minister
here
not knowing
what
five or ten
years will

bring
what will
endure
for all your sacrifices.

And Jeremiah
says
I was duped
and I let
myself
be duped.
I said,
"*I will say*
His name
no more.
But it
was like
a fire
burning
within me,
imprisoned
in my bones." (Jeremiah 20:9)

Your passion
for God's
people
for His
poor
is imprisoned
in your bones.
As Paul says
you are here
because
the love of God
has been
poured out
in our hearts
through the
Holy Spirit

who has been given us.
Your poverty,
as well as your insecurity,
is your treasure,
your faith.
You have
come to that part
of the journey
in which
you proclaim
that from your
roots to the past
the only
true liberation
is to serve —
to serve the community
by living the community
charism
by calling the council
to rediscover
the charism,
by calling
each Sister
to accountability
for your
community life together,
by calling
each Sister
for involvement
in vocation ministry.
You call
each Sister
to corporate
ministry
in the tradition
of your
community
to social injustice
and the cause

of the poor.

Peace is the message
of Jesus today,
a gift of healing
a gift of Himself.
St. John
says that
as Jesus
hung
on the cross
He bowed
His head
and handed
over
His Spirit,
and on Easter Sunday
John says
He burst in
upon the twelve
and said
to them:
"*Peace be with you...*
Receive the Holy Spirit." (John 20:21-22)
Today
He hands
over
His Spirit
to you.

You are not afraid
to pledge
the poverty
of insecurity.
Don't be afraid
  to vow obedience
to the dream
that was
given to this

diocese
over one hundred
years ago
by Sisters
who called
themselves
women of Providence —
women of caring
providing
    God.
Your very name
demands trust
and dependence
on the Spirit
to lead
and you to follow.

We, the Church, God's people,
    know you
    accept you
    acknowledge you
    and demand of you
    that you be
    Women of Providence.

IV

AGAINST MERRIMACK SKIES

TO care first

Invocation
State Senate of New Hampshire
June 1, 1993

Gracious God,
we have spent
this weekend
remembering.

We have honored
our dead
and as the
lingering notes
of taps
breezed across
their graves,
we heard
the stirring
trumpet sound
demanding
we march again
with new purpose
in our land.

You have given us the
gift of courage
to make us
bold
in the face of our
worst enemy — indifference.

Seal into our
souls
the firm resolve
not to falter
or wander
in aimless
indecision
but worthy
of our past
by confronting
the issues

of our day.

You give us
wisdom
that we might
understand
that decisions
cannot be made
without anguish.
If they are,
they are simple
edicts
and of no benefit
to the common good.

Fire in us
the gift of
right judgment
and firm us
in the midst of tension
and conflict
to seek
the dignity of
every human person
and we will
be secure
that our cause is just.

Move your spirit
through hearings
briefings, debating,
voting
and
cast aside all
hollow rhetoric.

Bring these
men and women
who enact

the laws of our state
to the realization
that the test
  of their worth
lies not in these
  halls
or in public acclaim
but in their own homes.

Remind them that it is
  there
that their integrity
is fashioned and tested.
Create in them
the power to care first,
  in kindness and love
for their families,
and all of us
will trust them
  to speak on
our behalf.

May these men and women
live the words of
  Micah,
the prophet,
"*This is what is required of*
  you,
to act with justice
to love tenderly and
to walk humbly with your
  God." (Micah 6:8)
Bless these men and women
  that they may not fizzle
at the end
of this session
like the Red Sox do
  every year.

# of singular commitment

Guardian Angel Parish
Berlin, New Hampshire
1993

Berlin, New Hampshire,
is not an isolated valley
hidden, tucked
amid the splendor
of Coos County
mountains.

In its obscurity
is a renowned city —
its fame
due not to industry
or influence;
its glory
is its people.

A steadfast faith
was nurtured here by
hundreds of men and women
who heard
the gentle, insistent
voice of Christ
demand they leave
all things
and follow Him.

Chiseled into
the character
of the people
of this north country
is a generosity
in Gospel living
that sets no boundaries.

In 1992
Guardian Angel Parish
celebrated
75 years of unstinting
service to the Church

and its global mission.

The Sisters of Charity
 of St. Hyacinth
returned on that occasion
to give thanks to this
 faith community
for the hundreds of women
 who left here
 to join them
in their mission
to be sign of the compassion
 of Christ
to broken lives.

They dedicate
this plaque then
to a parish of singular
commitment to Church vocation
 and thereby honor
all the men and women
who, inspired and fired
by the faith they witnessed here,
brought the good news of salvation
to almost every continent
 of the globe
 and certainly
to every parish and city
 of our state.

And to fix in memory
 and history
Monsignor Omer Bousquet,
who articulated the call
 of Christ for many
and lived it for all
 in total
priestly dedication
 to his people.

Ange Gardien,
stand vigilant
over this city
    and its people.

With unflinching care,
    watch over
its sons and daughters
who teach the way
    of Jesus Christ,
in season and out,
all over the world.

The children's window

St. Charles Church
Meredith, New Hampshire
October 2, 1995

Surely,
a church
on the shores
of a shimmering
lake
should have
a window
of the fishermen
casting out
their nets.
At least
one would expect
a sparkling
depiction of the Eucharist,
a dynamic
crucifixion
or a glorious
resurrection.
But here, the first
stained glass
window is of
the children.
It is a startling
surprise.

And yet, it reveals
more of our
human and divine
mystery
than is first evident.
The splash
of colors
highlights
a gentle
but preoccupied
Jesus.

Notice, too,

the children
radiant and
full of hope.
Yet,
there is no
pretense of fantasy
here.
Shadows of pain
linger
in the eyes
of the little ones
and are mirrored
back
into the Savior's
gaze.

Ah! This is what
the hidden
story of the
children's window reveals:
Our God
is not afraid
of our pain.
He embraces it
and cradles
our poor brokenness.

This unbridled love
is the reason
for Eucharist,
the answer to His cross,
the promise of resurrection.
His love
is the mystery revealed
in the children's
window.

Let us pray:

The children,
    Lord,
we bring
the children
to your loving care,
as You have commanded us.

Look
with love upon them.
They are so vulnerable,
surrounded by so many
    hurts and evils
only Your staying hand
can protect them.
And yet, happiness
is their inheritance
    of grace.

Flood their minds
    and hearts
    and souls
with joy.
Make them feel
    secure
and trusting.

Bless their parents
and all who help
    them
know and love You better.
We make our prayer in
    Christ, our Lord.

The consuming consent

Advent Reflection
Welcoming Ceremony
Thursday, November 30, 1989

We greet you, Mary,
a young pregnant girl
journeying through
spring fields and meadows
to visit an aged cousin.
The cradled life
  within you
hears the soft sound
  of your humming,
and now and then,
your tired sighs.

He easy rides
the lithesome beat
  of your footfall
  and yawns
within your womb
in cuddled contentment.

Je vous salue, Marie.

In the reverie of
  your waiting
Advent is an
awesome time for us —
of deep silences
  and great voids,
musing within us
  the Nicodemus
  puzzle,
"*What does it mean*
to be born again?" (John 3:4)

Bleak December dusks
  shiver us
into the lonesomeness
  of not being.
Then we are

jolted
with the realization
that even before sinew,
cell
or
tissue,
the gift
of God sparks
life
and we
become.

Then enclosed
before
limb or feature
our
story is
enfolded
in the core of soul —
we have identity
and we
are known
even before
womb-knitting
and are called
to hear glad tidings
of great joy.

Mere de Dieu,
we walk with you
again
in Advent
time
into the holiness
of life
and the splendor
of our call
to be
to be graced

to be disciple.
We greet you
as you fling
to Judean skies
your confident
reply,
"*I am the servant*
of the Lord." (Luke 1:38)

Singe our hesitant
hearts
with the same
consuming consent —
His will be done
in us.
And let our whole being
magnify the Lord with you.

Let all unholy fear
take flight
as we confess
with the angel's
words to you,
"*Nothing is impossible*
with God." (Luke 1:37)

Je vous salue, Marie.

You set the whole world spinning.
With shy and perky
curtsy,
you confound
the haughty and the mighty.

You know our fears.
You were troubled
by Gabriel's
invitation
to bear

    the Messiah.

You lure us
with your startled
"*How can this be?*" (Luke 1:34)
It is a good excuse
    for us
who seek escape
    lines
in all our dialogs
    with God.
But then you
    entrap us,
    beguiling us
with, "*Do whatever He tells you,*" (John 2:5)
    and water
    turns to wine
in the merriment
    of our chase
    to be like you
touched by God's
    joyful grace.

Je vous salue, Marie,
Mere de Dieu.
Through
you the Word
    becomes flesh
and frozen skies
    are luminous
with dazzling stars,
    and music
trumpets,
"*Glory to God,*" (Luke 2:14)
and a weary world
    rejoices.

Soar your prayers
above the ages

and roll them
against snow-peaked
  mountains,
echoing down
  ravines
of deep, dark forests,
and whisper them
into our inner
  timorous
  noise
and make us
  stilled
  defenseless
in your challenge.

Steel us
with your courage.
Set God's
  design
  free
  in us
and generation
  after generation
will know the mighty deeds
He has done for us.

Pleine de grace.
How you'd love
these forests, lakes,
cities, villages,
ocean, mountains
where the grandeur
  of your God
is forever etched!

You'd understand
  the faith
of this people,
granite solid,

ridged and forged
to the Rock of Peter.

As we, the Church
   in New Hampshire,
stand at the brink
   of the three-thousandth
   jubilee
of our redemption
   by Your Son,
ignite once more
   the fire within
us to be heralds
   of cross
and resurrection.

Make us
celebrate
the real memory,
the full mystery,
the total witness
   of His enduring love
   for us.

The Beautiful Bride on the Corner

St. John Neumann Church
Merrimack, New Hampshire
February 8, 1997

From nowhere
she appeared,
    lost amid
merging lanes,
traffic jams,
    stores
and arches.

She steps
up and out now
    and takes
    her place
front and center
    stage
to loud applause,
    everyone
    marveling
at her newfound
    beauty.

See how she basks
in the adulation.
She is the center
    of attention;
everyone
notices her
    now.

And yet,
she retains
a shy mystique,
    an appealing
and hidden beauty
    that draws
and charms us
into deeper
mysteries.

She lures us
with her young
  radiance
to seek
  old traditions
  and ageless
  truths.

With vivacious
  spontaneity
and magnificat
  exuberance
she lilts
  like
a melody of bells
spilling out against
Merrimack skies,
"*Behold the servant*
  of the Lord," (Luke1:38)
  and awes
with startled
  surprise
in her clear, confident
  voice
bursting with
captivating joy,
  weary souls
with the astounding news,
"*The Word becomes*
  flesh
  here
in this holy ground." (John 1:14)

She is the bride
  bedecked
  adorned
  with many
splendid jewels.
But then,

she fades
like the shy
little bishop
whose name she
bears
that we might
be enraptured by her spouse,
THE CHRIST,
bonded with him
in covenant
to be His
faithful people
and His household.

O proud, lovely,
new St. John Neumann Church,
be blest
with your patron's
grace — humility
and proclaim
in jubilee,
in and through
the next millennium,
"*My soul magnifies the Lord,*
my spirit rejoices in God, my Savior." (Luke 1:46-47)

Godspeed!

The solid conviction

St. Joseph Parish
Woodsville, New Hampshire
May 17, 1997

St. Joseph
is a great
patron
for a church
in Woodsville.
A carpenter,
he worked
with wood,
knew its texture
  its potential
  its endurance
  its practicality.

He must
have made
  a cradle
for the Christ
Child,
  a table
and all
the things
that turn
  a house
into a home.

Later Jesus
would work
with him
in his shop
and still later
He would die
on the wood
that would
redeem us all.

Wood
is a good
symbol

for your church.
It is fashioned
    from it.
It has withstood
    the seasons.
It has welcomed
    the joyful
    the weary
    the pleading
for a hundred
    years.

Wood is a good
    analogy
for you
parishioners.
You have
endured,
have made your
faith real and
    practical.
You know the
texture
    of the needs
of your
community
and you have
    walked
    always
hammered to
the solid
conviction
    that you
    would reach
your full
potential
if you believed.

You have been

craftsmen and
women
  who have
  fashioned
a wonderful
  model
of faith,
  taught
  learned
  lived
and celebrated.

May God
continue
to form you as
His
faithful people.

In the Hollow

Our Lady of Fatima Church
New London, New Hampshire
December 7, 1997

Like a shy
little girl
she used
to hide herself.

She lived
in a beautiful
hollow
and was
embarrassed
by the splendor
that surrounded
her.
She thought
herself
too plain
and practical
to be noticed.
In spring
flowers
danced in
her meadows
and whiffed
fresh
perfumes
like
swinging urns
of incense
all around her.

She loves
music.
It animates
her
and gives
dance
to her soul.
So she delights

in summer.
Peals of laughter
and joyous
family sounds
capture
all that
she yearns to be.
But she worries
that she
suffocates.
She strained to
burst through
her own limits
and soar above
oppressive
inadequacies
and fling
into summer's
joyful leisure
and reflective play
souls
anxious
to breathe
the depths
of God's
Spirit.

October
always
dazzled her.
The mountains
blazed
and she blushed.
Her patched
clothes
fixed her
between
astonishing
skies

of startling
  rising
and setting
  suns
and the endless
  grandeur
that reveals
  only
the penetrating
  beauty
of the ever
  creating God.

Winter
accented
  her lack.
Snows
  whirled
in whistling
  leaps around her
but she
could offer
  little warmth
and invited
  no cozy
hearth of comfort
to those stung
by the barrenness
of the winter
indifference
that crept
  into
their lives,
their marriages,
their love of God.
Now
in mid-stride
she changed.
She's more confident,

more alluring
and has drawn
into her own
    personality
the splendor
    that
once dominated her.

She is now Spring.
The scents
    and sounds
of fresh beginnings
engulf her.
"*Behold*
I make all
things new" (Revelations 21:5)
is her hymn
of promise
    and challenge.

She is Summer,
a silent sentinel
that lures
us in to ponder.
A quiet, cool
place
where playful
mix of color
and crystal,
wood and
texture
make
all things holy.
"*Whatever you do,*
whether in speech
or in action,
do it in the name
of the Lord Jesus.
Give thanks to God

the Father through
Him." (Letter to the Colossians 3:17)

She is Autumn,
drawing
into herself
the splendor splashed
all around her
sanctifying it
and flinging
praise of God's
majesty
out to the
mountains
and the valleys.
"*My soul proclaims*
the greatness of God.
My spirit rejoices
in God, my Savior." (Luke 1:46-47)

She is the inscape
of winter.
Her snows
now
are comfort
that mantle
her
and she in turn
embracing
pain
billows
blizzards
of grace
to those
trapped
in the
harshness
of frozen
hopes.

She welcomes,
  warmed with
a Christed mandate:
"*Come to me*
all you who
find life weary
and I will
refresh you.
Learn of me
for I am meek
and humble of
heart." (Matthew 11:28-29)

Not so long ago
  in Portugal
Mary came to
  a hollow
and spoke with
  little children.

You have
  redesigned
in your hollow
this holy place.
You take
all the elements
of grace and nature,
embellish them,
  and in prayer
  and sacrifice
offer them
  to God.
May God
hold you
in the hollow
  of His hand
and hallow
  everything
  you do.

To the Heights of Hope

Invocation
Inauguration
Governor Jeanne Shaheen
January 9, 1997

Gracious God,
you give us
this noon ceremony
   to remind us
we need not wait
till Sunday to be assured
that New England Patriots
are victorious.

To this gathering
come today
men and women
seeking Your blessings
   as they begin
a year of service
to "we the people"
of New Hampshire.
Bless them
with the gift of silence
for these men and women
who write, judge, or execute
   our laws
must first of all listen.
All speech is babble,
all debate confused,
all proclamations null,
until the voice of the powerless
   the cry for justice
   the thundering protest
   against violence
are heard.

Here, in this chamber
there must be silence
so that our Constitution
may whisper guidance
and Your Holy Spirit
break through the barriers

of clashing noise
and lead
to the quiet task
of righteous discernment.

May these men and women
who are the voice of the
people
accept the burden
of becoming
and remaining
listeners.

Gracious God,
bless our governor.
Sustain and strengthen her
for weariness is
the partner
of responsibility;
criticism,
the companion of leadership;
and negativism,
often the catalyst
of action.

Grant her the gift of
confidence
which empowers her
to burst through
the security of inaction
and fear of renewal
that paralyzes
and holds us captive
to indifference.

Grant her
a heart of joy,
courageous enough
to pierce the gloom

of doubt
and empower her
to rally all of us
to the heights of hope.

Bless this woman
who takes
her place in history today —
not so much because
she is a first
but because
she comes
to dedicate
all her strength
all her talent
her whole person
to accept
once more
the enduring
but often forgotten
biblical
and constitutional
truth:
There is no power
but the power to serve
and all other power
is ultimately chaos.

Bless this generous
woman.
May her husband
and her children
sustain and strengthen her
and be her healing
and her consolation.

Lord, make all of us
remember
that life is like traveling on

101 East.
"It's a trip,"
as they say,
trying to figure
which way
the pieces fit together
where the road goes,
and how it gets there
wandering about
like me
when I pray.

But I bet everyone,
even before
it's done,
as they move away
the cranes,
will sit bumper to bumper
and say,
"I told you we needed
four more lanes."
Enough is never enough
so we'll complain
(sort of like me
when I pray).
No wonder God
unfolds His constructions,
makes His interconnections
without our consultations
except, of course,
in His prayer.
(Thy will be done.)

The surprise
of all God's startling
symmetry
is that we're the masterpiece
and all is grace.
Thank God for prayer!

V

Resonating Songs

old st. mary's

St. Mary of the Assumption
Haydenville, Massachusetts
1989

Around a curve,
up the gentle slope
of a hill,
we suddenly
come upon you,
St. Mary's,
Haydenville.

Cars whiz
by
but you stand
unperturbed
and permanent,
a lovely
prayer by the
side
of the road.

You think
you're unnoticed
but your shadow
has cast
a century of blessings
upon thousands
of travelers,
lured by your
presence
into silent
reflection.

You stand
with such elegant
grace
and dazzle us
with your peace.

The sun
splashes a myriad of color

on your arches
from windows
stained by
history as much
as art.

And high above
your altar
is the crown of your
beauty,
the chancel
window
of Mary's
Assumption.

Old St. Mary's,
ever
draw our
eyes
to this Lady
for which
you are named.

Radiant
and triumphant
she shouts
to us,
"Have faith.
You will endure!

"Think of those
gone before
you —
their grief
their floods
their bitter poverty.
Have hope.
They, like me,
have triumphed.

So will you!"

This is our church
nestled in
the Berkshire foothills —

A citadel —

And more —
the home
of our prayer.

Old St. Mary's
ever young
fortify
sustain
strengthen
us.

Be a tender mother
to your sons
and daughters —
their comfort
their hope
their sure refuge
for another
one hundred years.

spires against the sky

Diocese of Manchester Museum
St. Anne's Church
April 22, 1990

Eternal God,
You create
time and seasons
  and design
our pilgrimage
  through them
to You.

Here in the museum
we create a
sacred place
  to weave
in the fabric
  of faith
the story of
  that journey.

These books
  and records,
this art
  and these artifacts,
these photographs
  and mementos,
haunt our memories
  with the reality
of men and women
  who
  flung
magnificent spires
against the sky;

who, from vowed
  or family
poverty,
gave us
a rich heritage
  of education
  health care

and compassionate
    service
to your poor.

We are confident
    of the future
because of our past.
When with
    swift grace
you riven
    our world
or our lives
with saving power,
may our response
be generous
    and quick
    and transforming
that your
    word
may live
    dynamic,
    demanding
among
    the dust
    the clutter
    and the treasure
of what we are.

Reed of God

Reed of God,
not shaken by the wind or rain,
alone, among the beaten grain
  that falls
  and crawls,
tumbling to the earth,
victim of the wind's tyrannical mirth.
Reed of God,
if this is true,
why is it said of you,
"*You leapt*!" (Luke 1:41)
at the whispering melody
of her who is God's eternal Breeze?
Reed of God,
make me like thee,
hard against the winds of man;
ah, but meek to her command
  who is eternally
the Breeze of God.

Beloved of God,
dreamer of royal seat,
with royal armies replete,
youth all afire
with passion fire
to win a Kindgom for the King.
Beloved of God,
"Behold your King,"
  they sing.
You, in defeat,
gaze upon His feet,
nailed, purpled, crucified.
Beloved of God,
make me like to thee.
Give unto me
the gift given unto thee
from Our King upon a tree,
for all eternity — Mary.

An abundant place

Lord, make this kitchen
a welcoming place.
Fill it with the fragrant smells
of appetizing food cooking
and with welcoming people
greeting all who come here
seeking friendship as well
as nourishment.

Lord, make this kitchen
an abundant place
where grace
gives subsistence,
laughter builds hope
and silence brings
us to reverent gratitude.

Lord, make this kitchen
a place of dignity
where every person
is celebrated as Your image.

Lord, fill this kitchen
with Your presence
and we will know peace.

Keene Community Kitchen
April 1992

unbent against the seasons

Mary Flynn
Tree Dedication
August 20, 1981
Stockbridge, Massachusetts

Oh God of loveliness,
we stand before
You
at the eventide
of the grandeur
and sparkling
beauty of
this day.

Let the meadows
sweep into our
souls
the gift of happiness
resonating songs
of winged flight
that sweep
across the security
of these fields.

Let the mountains
lift up our
spirits
and give us the courage
which comes
to the steadfast.

Give us the
deep tranquillity
of lakes
serenely calling
us
into Your peace
through
sun-splashed days.

And bless us
with this tree,
making us unbent

against
the seasons,
laughing
and dancing
in the delight of
wind and rain,
mantled in the snow,
embraced with the
merriment of children
and growing always
in the sound of music.

And may this tree
be lofty
and stately as the
lady it will honor.
We ask this blessing
Father, Son and Holy Spirit.

Against a chilling Night

October 1994

Shepherds
 wrapped
in their
own fears
 against
a chilling night
were lured
from their isolation
by whisperings
in the night
to visit
a cave
and see
in a manger
 a new mystery.

Music filled
the night
and stars
almost touched
frozen hills
as they returned
 glorifying God.

Christmas
challenges
our loneliness
and invalidates
 our exile.

None of our fears
 are personal,
nor is our isolation
 lasting.
God has embraced
 us.

An aura of elegance

Martha Tilove
Washington, D.C.
January 1996

Martha,
lingering images
of hospitality
echo in
our memory
of you.

A welcoming
woman,
without fuss,
setting
a table
for conversation
and withdrawing
into rapt attention
to contemplate
our words
and listen
to our silence.

Martha,
a woman
comfortable
with the mess
of life,
restless
with its questions,
serene about
its doubts.

An aura
of elegance
followed her.
Sharp wit
and tender grace
clothed her.

When fears

closed in
her only escape
    was love,
the only home
any of us have,
the only destiny
we share.

Martha,
may your
rest be as deep
as the snows
of this unusual winter,
nurturing
quietly
our earth
with the
energy
of spring
which will
surprise us
again with
bursting life
and fragile beauty
and turn
the memory
    of you
again
into
reality
of a living
presence
among us.

Heart speaks to Heart

Colleen McCaffery
March 1997

The snow
came
in silence,
shrouded us
in sorrow,
demanding
we walk
softly
speak tenderly,
and mourn
our unsobbed tears.

A little girl
whose name
is speckled
with impish beauty
has left us.

Frigid fields
and our own
frozen emotions
give us
no comfort.

The earth is
too barren
to console.

We look up to you,
our God.
Permit, in your grace,
Colleen
to smite us
with her bravery.

Allow her
to sweep past
the barriers of voice

with words
too weak
to pierce our grief.
Let her speak
    in silence,
the lover's art,
and hold in
captivating love
hearts as broken
    as ours.

Colleen,
lilt the music
of your tantalizing
    courage,
your rituals,
    of dolls and plays,
your serene
    security
of being home
    into the drab
expanse
of our
sudden emptiness.
Surprise
us again
with wonder
and awe
and the joy
of simple
    little
charming things.
You live forever.
Help us to live
    now.

May God
guide your doctors
and nurses
as they care
for you.

May His grace
strengthen and
console you,
ease your pain
of mind and body
and keep you in
His love
in Christ, our Lord.
Amen.

A Blessing for the Sick

Prayer Card
August 9, 1996

A prayer for Healing

Prayer Card
August 9, 1996

Lord, you healed
many people.
Look upon me.
  See
my fears,
my pain,
my loneliness,
and touch me
with Your love
that I may find
Your healing power
in my mind and body.

May Mary,
the Mother of Your Son,
intercede on my behalf
that I may find
  in You
comfort, compassion
  and courage.
I ask this in
Christ, our Lord.
Amen.

The stealthful invasion

Easter 1994

The seldom times
  we have
to be surprised
  by spring
is reason to believe
in Resurrection.

Violence
marches free rein
across all borders
even those of
our own hearts.
But evil
cannot stop
the stealthful
  invasion
of April greens
on meadow and mountain.

The rat-a-tat-tat
  of hatred
  hammers
new crosses
on the weary landscape
  of souls
  too young
to abandon
  spirits
into hands
as pierced as theirs.

No wonder!
We have filled
their imagery
with bunnies,
  eggs,
and an
array of promises

that any pain
can be smashed;
pledges we make
to them
like flowers
withering
before revealing
"The seed must die
before it produces
much life."

Alleluias
do not hippety-hop
over empty tombs.
They rumble
in doubt caverns
of death's victory
before they burst to life.

"*It is finished*" (John 19:30)
is their first uncertain note,
wrenched from a throat
parched with fear
of claustrophobic
boulders
blocking escape
into surrender
to a freer
destiny.

The crescendo
of alleluias
is lifted
on the triumph
of the encompassing
cry of Jesus
to accept
the death failure

of the human perspective
and to lift
all creation
beyond our
own
boundaries
into the
destiny of God.

Alleluias
force us
to Easter hunts.
Brightly colored
eggs,
or fields, or flowers
are not such search.
The anguish
we carry
needs more meaning.
"*It is finished*"
is our beginning.

Alleluia!

from Route 291

Sacred Heart Church
Springfield, Massachusetts
1985

You boldly stand there
on the corner
like some young girl
blushing
at her own beauty.

Shame on you
at your age
You should be fading
into some quiet background
content
with responsibility
satisfied
with reverence
Not out there on the corner
competing with younger
women for ohs and ahs
of admiration.

Don't you know
everybody in the city
is talking about you.

What right do you have
at your age
to be gathering to yourself
so many new and
beautiful people
whose melodic languages
swirl around you
with such charm
whose dark
and flashing eyes
spark with wonder
and delight
as they murmur
new endearments
to your regal grace

Oh Que Linda! Que Bonita!
mi iglesia!

More power to you
grand old lady
flaunting your beauty
and
dazzling us
with elegance.
The sight of you
on a spring morning
with April greens
and cherry blossoms
dancing
at your side
lilts new songs
and beguiles us
with the promise
that ageless beauty
does endure.

Stay always young
Sacred Heart Church
for us who ride
Route 291
luring us
with your beauty
your undaunted spirit
your incredible youth.

Be for us a sign of our Church
bursting forever with spring
rose tinting sunsets
with dreams completed
and dawns with new prophecies
and promises to be fulfilled.

Above the splendor

St. Michael's Cathedral
Springfield, Massachusetts
September 30, 1997

This is a fitting
   cathedral
for Michael.
It towers
   solid
in the center of things.
Traffic hectically
in fits
and starts
crawls impatiently
before it.

Impressive
   buildings
of art, literature
   and science
surround it.
There are more graceful,
   loftier churches,
but this is for Michael
whose rallying cry
is, "Who is like to God?"

Michael's cathedral
   must pull us
above the splendor
   and the grandeur
   of cities
established here
into higher realms
where God's inestimable
   beauty dwells,
for Michael protects
   the holiness
   of God
and ours as well.

See how this silent citadel,

powerfully entrenched,
gently lifts us up.
The sweeping lawn,
    elegant trees,
the wide approach,
the new terrace,
the ordinary but
    splendid doors
    that dominate
and bid welcome,
the Michael statue,
the cross lifted high
all proclaim protection
that sweeps across
our inner fears
and haunting doubts.

Now Cathedral Square
    completes the Quadrangle.
The cloistered walk,
the surprising gardens,
the home and church
    of bishops,
the worry and work of
    ministry,
the newest technology,
and our oldest prayers
    are met here.
Here the four counties
    are joined
and find their transcendent
identity and unity.
The holy oils
and sacred charism
are sent forth from here
to heal, restore, empower
and gather all our good
    works

to be sanctified
and made pleasing
to the Lord.

The Cathedral of Springfield
rooted
in tradition and grace
intensifies within us
the mission
to be
one and holy
Catholic and apostolic;
in witnessing
we are disciples
of the crucified and risen
Lord.

The cathedral confronts us:
we are many;
we must become one.
The cathedral teaches,
for here is the bishop's
chair,
but we all must evangelize.
The cathedral celebrates,
but we all offer
the perfect sacrifice.
The cathedral consecrates,
and we are set apart
to serve the poorest of the
poor among us.

Michael, Archangel,
patron of our cathedral
church,
dedicate
and defend us
to these tasks.

My parish

1978

Holds sacred memories for
me —
the moments when God
touched me
with His grace
at Eucharist
when he refreshed a weary pilgrim
at His table.

I stood with confidence
and vowed to cherish
and honor and love
another
as a sign of His love
for all mankind.
I can remember the awesome
smell of incense,
the thundering songs
the men sang
at the close of a powerful
mission.

I've wept in this church;
come home to bury
here my dead.
I've held in my arms
my firstborn
to receive the eternal gift
of life.
I've knelt here and, ashamed,
admitted guilt and failure
and felt the power of healing
and forgiveness
and the exulting knowledge
that God loves me.

My parish is more than memory;
it is a gift of God.

The soul's Triumph

Meditation on the Crucifix
at Mont Marie
September 21, 1995

Crucified Jesus,
I kneel
lost in this vast chapel
where there is
no cozy escape
from my inner confusions.
I look up to you
but you are turned from me.
Other images of you
on your cross
show your
head bent,
listening to and healing
our pain.

Here in this
chapel
your face is
flung to the
skies
and as I look
upon you,
I am haunted
by the words,
"*A death He*
freely accepted."

(Eucharistic Prayer II)

How can I
surrender to such
unknowns?
I cannot even accept
my life.
How welcome its end?
My sins, my fears,
my loneliness I wrestle with,
begging you to take
from me
my inner self, my limits.

The barriers to my peace,
    the dyings
I cling to
    block me
from resurrection.

Teach me to accept
    myself
living in you
now, as in the end,
which is the beginning
    of my yearning;
to love you
    above all loves.
Then, my other
    will be
eternally secure.

Bless this community
of women religious
    and its leaders.
May the prayer,
joyous service
    and pain
offered here
give You
honor and praise
    and glory
forever.

Shafts of light
    crisscross
around your crucified
    image.
Radiate
    these beams
into our souls
    that we might
have your courage

    and in you
find our triumph.

Then, we will
    shout
in victory:
"It is finished
in Christ, our Lord!"

"...And with a sword he clove my breast,

Plucked out the heart he made beat higher,

And in my stricken bosom pressed

Instead a coal of LIVING FIRE..."

From "The Prophet," by Alexander Pushkin, 1826

NOTRE DAME COLLEGE

2321 Elm Street, Manchester, New Hampshire 03104